DEAN MARTIN, who would have been 100 this year, embraces Frank Sinatra.

LIFE

CW01669701

THE RAT PACK

THE ORIGINAL BAD BOYS

BY JAMES KAPLAN

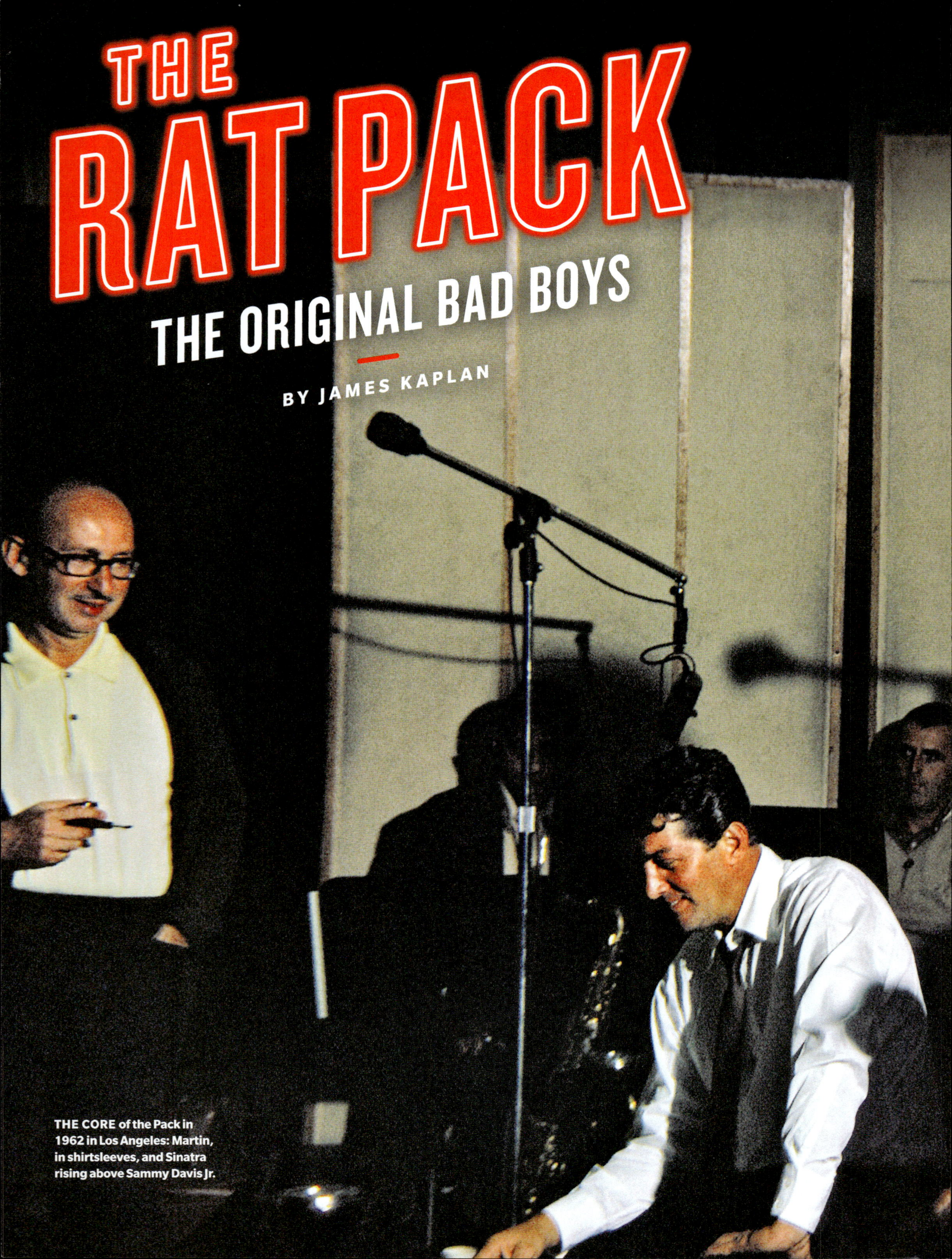

THE CORE of the Pack in 1962 in Los Angeles: Martin, in shirtsleeves, and Sinatra rising above Sammy Davis Jr.

LIFE

THE RAT PACK
THE ORIGINAL BAD BOYS

Special thanks: Brad Beatson, Melissa Frankenberry, Kristina Jutzi, Simon Keeble, Seniqua Koger, Kate Roncinske, Kristen Zwicker

Published by LIFE Books, an imprint of Time Inc. Books, 225 Liberty Street New York, NY 10281

Vol. 17, No. 10 • May 26, 2017

We welcome your comments and suggestions about LIFE Books. Please write to us at:
LIFE Books, Attention: Book Editors
P.O. Box 62310
Tampa, FL 33662-2310

If you would like to order any of our hardcover Collector's Edition books, please call us at 800-327-6388, Monday through Friday, 7 a.m.–9 p.m. Central Time.

Front cover: On January 27, 1961, in Manhattan, the core Pack members—Dean Martin, Sammy Davis Jr. and Frank Sinatra—enjoy smokes, as well as one another, backstage at Carnegie Hall after performing at a benefit in honor of Dr. Martin Luther King Jr. PHOTOGRAPH FROM BETTMANN/GETTY

Page I: PHOTOGRAPH BY JOHN DOMINIS/LIFE/THE PICTURE COLLECTION

Pages 2-3: PHOTOGRAPH FROM MICHAEL OCHS ARCHIVES/GETTY

These pages: PHOTOGRAPH BY ALLAN GRANT/LIFE/THE PICTURE COLLECTION

Back cover: PHOTOGRAPH BY FLOYD MCCARTY/MPTVIMAGES

SINATRA, MARTIN (far right) and others (that's Debbie Reynolds right behind Sinatra) at the Copa circa 1960.

INTRODUCTION

A RING-A-DING MOMENT IN TIME

What happened in Vegas didn't stay in Vegas, that's for sure. It couldn't have. These guys, particularly Frank Sinatra but also Dean Martin and Sammy Davis Jr., were just too big at that precise moment—which was a very brief moment indeed if we are speaking of the period when the so-called Rat Pack was intact and creating its legend. If Sinatra, Martin and Davis and their pals were making news in Vegas with their outrageous behavior, well, that news would spread. The booze, the women, the crazy shows at the Sands, all those gangsters around—and Jack Kennedy, too. And then they went and made the movie and the whole country starts going, "Eee-O Eleven, Eee-O Eleven," and everyone in Paducah is getting a look at those glittering casinos, those citadels of sin.

No: There was no way this was going to stay in Vegas.

CBS/GETTY

It rolled out of the desert like tumbleweed. It grew larger—as a story, as an idea—and became distorted. The gossip columnists in Hollywood and New York loved the stuff, and of course made the stuff better. Quite quickly, it was impossible to say what had really happened and what hadn't, who was in and who was out, who was a bigger lush, Frankie-Boy or Dino Martini. All that was certain was that there was a helluva lot of fun being had by the guys, and their many fans were living vicariously through the tales, tall tales and true ones.

Remarkably, though the Rat Pack of Sinatra, Martin, Davis, Peter Lawford and Joey Bishop was a fleeting and ephemeral thing—and wasn't even called the Rat Pack (the real Rat Pack, as you will soon learn, was Humphrey Bogart's earlier club)—its mythos has endured down the decades. We at LIFE thought it was high time, after more than half a century, to put together a visual history of just what happened. (Pictures, after all, are incapable of lying.) We found in our own archives wonderful material from LIFE's storied shooter John Dominis, as we expected to, and then we cast the net wider.

We realized quickly that this story needed an authoritative, lively narrative—one as fine and entertaining as a Sinatra song with a Nelson Riddle arrangement. Novelist and biographer James Kaplan came quickly to mind. His 2010 book, *Frank: The Voice,* was rightly acclaimed, and the memoir he co-wrote with Jerry Lewis about Lewis's relationship with Martin was also terrific. Kaplan knew this terrain well, and was eager to revisit it for us and for our readers. He flew west, and brought back the story that threads its way through these pages.

You're going to come to know these people: the entertainers and impresarios, the mobsters and their molls, those who tried to draw close to Sinatra's flame and those who ran away—or were cast away. This is a big, sexy blast from the past, and now the band begins to play.

SID AVERY/MPTVIMAGES

WHICH PHOTOGRAPH from 1960 represents the real Rat Pack? On the opposite page, we have the boys behaving well and smiling pleasantly: From left, Frank Sinatra, Dean Martin, Sammy Davis Jr., Peter Lawford and Joey Bishop.

On this page, we have Davis, Martin, Sinatra and Bishop engaging in fisticuffs, which might well have occured with this gang. But it turns out this, too, is playacting, as they stage a scene for their first film together, *Ocean's Eleven*.

THE DATES of many of the photos on these pages are going to be "circa," not least because many of the photographers back then were just shooting, not taking great notes as they bent elbows in various ways, and these days people are still figuring out when the guys pictured might have been together—as here, at the Sands—at a given point in time. So then: Circa 1960, we have cavorting, from left, Dean, Peter, Sammy, Frank, Joey—and (we're pretty sure) the character actor Buddy Lester, who was part of the gang in that year's film *Ocean's Eleven.* As well as any, this active, fun-filled moment can be seen as the summit of the Summit.

BOB WILLOUGHBY/MPTVIMAGES

THE SUMMIT OF SOMETHING

BY JAMES KAPLAN

"This is the West, sir. When the legend becomes fact, print the legend."

—*The Man Who Shot Liberty Valance* (1962)

The line is from an old movie about myth and reality in the Old West, but it might as well have been written about a legend that was born a half century ago in Las Vegas, a town whose own myth has shimmered like a mirage on the high Nevada desert for as long as anyone alive can remember. The legend is the sometimes true, often highly imaginative story of the Rat Pack.

We will get to truth and fiction presently, but first, like the newspaperman in John Ford's *The Man Who Shot Liberty Valance,* we must acknowledge the very real power of legends. They compel us, they stir us, they fill our dreams and guide our behavior. The idea of the Rat Pack was born at a hinge of time in the American consciousness, a moment between the conformism of the '50s and the chaos of the '60s, an eye-blink when the horrors and heroism of World War II were still in recent memory (and nuclear fear underlay every diversion), when compensatory excess, in the form of sex, alcohol and cigarettes, was winked at and 20th-century ideals of manhood hadn't yet been subverted by the androgynous aesthetic of rock 'n' roll.

The Rat Pack was an idea even more than it was a reality. And though Frank, Dean and Sammy were three real men, their respective myths tend, to this day, to jostle reality aside. Throw in Joey Bishop and Peter Lawford as window dressing, or ballast, and you've got a sharkskin-suited, skinny-tied, chain-smoking, chain-drinking, Dionysian parade float. Watch it trundle down Main Street; cheer as it goes by. We won't see its like again. Even if it wasn't quite there in the first place.

Nineteen fifty-five—the year Albert Einstein, Charlie Parker, Wallace Stevens and James Dean died—was the year the Rat Pack was born, and Dean, Sammy, Joey and Peter were nowhere near it yet. Frank was, just. The birthplace was in Holmby Hills, an exclusive enclave of West Los Angeles just off Sunset Boulevard, in the big white house on South Mapleton Drive that belonged to the 56-year-old Humphrey Bogart and his young wife, Lauren Bacall.

Bogart was a renowned consumer of alcohol ("The whole world is three drinks behind," he used to say) and a notorious rebel when it came to all things Hollywood. Unlike most movie stars, he didn't like to go out much, couldn't stand all the seeing-and-being-seen malarkey of Tinseltown, and so the world came to him—or at least that part of the world he considered amusing: such glittering old-Hollywood luminaries as Judy Garland and her husband, Sid Luft; the David Nivens; Spencer Tracy; Ira Gershwin; Rodeo Drive restaurateur Mike Romanoff and his wife, Gloria; Bogart's agent, Irving "Swifty" Lazar; and Frank Sinatra.

Sinatra, who was agonizingly insecure about many things—his height, his looks, his ethnicity, his lack of education and his blue-collar New Jersey background, for starters—"craved class the way a junkie craves the needle," in the words of his valet George Jacobs. And in Sinatra's eyes, Humphrey Bogart, who had grown up a rich boy in Manhattan, then spent the rest of his life living it down, was pure class. Sinatra idolized everything about the wry, disaffected Bogart, from the way he dressed (custom-made suits, shirts, shoes; sport jackets with pocket squares; fedoras from Cavanagh to cover his *(continued on page 14)*

"DEVIL MAY CARE" would have been the slogan of Humphrey Bogart's Rat Pack if it had adopted a slogan as well as an "official" slate of officers. In this photograph, made circa 1954 as the core of the Pack was coalescing, Bogie laughs large at Romanoff's in L.A. as Art Linkletter, of all people, shares some news. They are at a party following the premiere of mutual friend Judy Garland's gig with the Los Angeles Philharmonic. The shoulder to the right belongs to Lauren Bacall, Bogart's wife, and the lovely, smiling visage above to British actress Jean Simmons.

MURRAY GARRETT/GETTY

Rocket Richard
In Peak Form

RUE DES ARCHIVES/GRANGER

A LOVE STORY beyond Hollywood expectation or hope was that of Bogart and Bacall, seen here at home. He was a 45-year-old star in 1944 and she was a 19-year-old ingénue when they met on the set of *To Have and Have Not* and Bogie said presciently, "I just saw your test. We'll have a lot of fun together." A year later, after Bogart divorced his wife, the actors wed and set up housekeeping in an exclusive neighborhood in Holmby Hills. Their home became a hangout for Bogie's drinking buddies, not least because Bogart—as opposed to his young wife—preferred staying in to going out. He also preferred sailing to being on land and drinking to not drinking, but if these inclinations caused frictions, they were minor ones; "Bogart and Bacall" remains today a Tinseltown saga better, and happier, than most screenplays. As Den Mother, Betty Bacall was a happy host to the original Rat Pack, and as is well known, grew very close to fellow executive board member (and leader of its successor association) Frank Sinatra. On the following pages: Members of Bogie's Rat Pack, described in the accompanying official caption as "a group of exceedingly well heeled Bohemians that include screen stars and millionaires from Hollywood's super-ritzy Holmby Hills section . . . seen sitting at a table having cocktails at the Copa Room in Hollywood on October 15, 1956."

receding hairline), to the way he drank and smoked, to the cool irony that colored his world-view. Frank Sinatra was a hot character, with boiling emotions and a short fuse, and cool looked good to him. Unattainable, but good.

Sinatra had begun hanging around the Bogarts' house in the early '50s, when he was down on his luck: His singing and acting careers had stalled; he'd been dropped by Columbia Records, MGM Studios, even his agents; and his second wife, Ava Gardner, had left him for a bullfighter. Bogie and Bacall took him in—his disaffection with Hollywood matched theirs. As did his capacity for alcohol. By 1954, Sinatra had won an Oscar for his role in *From Here to Eternity* and had begun recording a series of genius albums with Nelson Riddle at Capitol Records, marking the greatest comeback in show-business history. Still, he continued drinking: Success held some demons at bay but also brought on new ones.

One late night (the story goes), when Bogart, Sinatra and some of the other usual suspects were lolling around the living room in the South Mapleton house, somewhat the worse for wear, Bacall, much younger than the rest and sharp-tongued, walked in and said, "My God—you all look like a rat pack."

Bogart liked that. In his usual spirit of irony, he proposed that those present form a semiofficial club under that name. "In order to qualify," Lauren Bacall wrote in her memoir *By Myself*, "one had to be addicted to nonconformity, staying up late, drinking, laughing and not caring what anyone thought or said about us . . . We held a dinner in a private room at Romanoff's to elect officials and draw up rules—Bogie's way of thumbing his nose at Hollywood. I was voted Den Mother, Bogie was in charge of public relations. No one could join without unanimous approval of the charter members . . . What fun we had with it all! We were an odd assortment, but we liked each other so much, and every one of us had a wild sense of the ridiculous. The press had a field day, but we had the upper hand."

The fun was short-lived, though, and ended, seemingly for good, with Humphrey Bogart's death from esophageal cancer in January 1957, at age 58. After a little while, Sinatra began dating Bogie's young widow; things turned serious, and he and Bacall came

AP

FROM LEFT: Bogart; producer Sid Luft; Bacall; Luft's wife, Judy Garland; Ellie Graham; Jack Entratter; restaurateur Mike Romanoff (partly hidden); Sinatra; Gloria Romanoff; David and Hjordis Niven.

close to marrying. But then, inevitably, the romance blew up. Sinatra, the swingingest bachelor of the late '50s (even as he and the Widow Bogart had considered matrimony, he was seeing close to a dozen other women), simply wasn't built for the "institute you can't disparage," as his 1955 hit song "Love and Marriage" somewhat ironically put it.

And so the original Rat Pack folded, and that would have been that, except that Hollywood has long been fond of remakes.

Though Sinatra was initially rocked by Bogart's death—he canceled all his performances at New York's Copacabana that week—he was very soon back to the business of being Frank Sinatra, which by the late 1950s was very big business indeed: There was his brilliant recording career (Sinatra was in the process of leaving Capitol and establishing his own record label, Reprise); his very busy nightclub practice; and the highly lucrative business of producing and starring in motion pictures. After proving his commercial and dramatic viability with *From Here to Eternity,* Sinatra soon set up his own production company; he also stayed very busy in front of the cameras, appearing in as many as three films per annum over the next few years. Trying to showcase his versatility (and stave off boredom), he made all kinds of pictures: dramas (*Suddenly, Young at Heart, Not As a Stranger, The Man with the Golden Arm*), comedy (*The Tender Trap*) and musicals (*Guys and Dolls, Pal Joey*). In 1958, he starred in the World War II movie *Kings Go Forth.* And later that year, he played a disillusioned veteran in the drama *Some Came Running.* His costars were Dean Martin and Shirley MacLaine.

Sinatra and Martin had first met when Frank introduced Dean and his partner, Jerry Lewis, to the audience at Martin and Lewis's Copacabana premiere in 1948. From 1946 to 1956, on TV, in the movies and in live performance, Dean and Jerry were the biggest thing in show business, while Frank's career crashed and then miraculously rose again. Yet nobody predicted a comeback for Dean Martin after the 1956 breakup of Martin and Lewis: The smart money bet that the multitalented Jerry would flourish and Dean, who was widely viewed as merely Lewis's straight man, would vanish.

Martin did flounder at first, but then, to the surprise of everyone (including himself), he landed a serious role alongside Marlon Brando in the 1958 World War II movie *The Young Lions* and drew rave reviews for his unexpected depths as a dramatic actor. His records had been selling pretty well since the Martin and Lewis days, but this one film positioned him to become a star in his own right.

In the meantime, Frank Sinatra had never stopped believing in him. The two men had hit it off from the beginning, for complex reasons. Though on the surface it would have seemed Sinatra and Martin had much in common—both were magnetic Italian-American singer/actors with swinging reputations—in fact, they were different in more ways than they were similar, and their differences interested each man. Sinatra was a molten cauldron of oversensitivity and insecurity; Martin was detached and ironic, imbued with a quality known in Italian as *menefreghismo*—in (polite) translation, "not giving a damn." Sinatra was short, slight and (by his own estimation) funny-looking; Martin was tall, strong and handsome, with an athlete's easy grace. He had huge hands (he had briefly boxed professionally and had worked as a card dealer) and was a close-to-scratch golfer. Perhaps most impressive of all his gifts—and most enviable to Sinatra—was a natural flair for comedy. Jerry Lewis had detected at the beginning of their partnership that Dean had a subtle, lightning-fast wit. And one of the things Frank Sinatra, who was almost incapable of ad-libbing a comic line onstage, desperately wanted to be was funny.

Sinatra envied and admired almost every one of Martin's innate qualities, almost to the point of idolatry. As for Dean's feelings about Frank—well, who knew? He certainly admired him as a singer. But in general, Martin was such (continued on page 22)

BOUND FOR VEGAS in the postwar years were two supposedly unrelated industries: entertainment and the mob. In this photograph, taken in 1945, the notorious Meyer Lansky poses on the construction site of the Flamingo hotel, which he helped develop, as did Bugsy Siegel and other bad guys. Lansky was an East Coast guy and Siegel was now L.A. Soon Bugsy—and Sinatra and Davis and all others who could sing or dance or crack wise—would be shuttling regularly between La-La Land and Las Vegas.

HY PESKIN

LAS VEGAS NEWS BUREAU

THE BIRTH OF VEGAS, **Part I. The photos on this and the next two pages depict an extraordinary city emerging from the unwelcoming dust of the desert. Today, as we know, Las Vegas is a pulsing urban center with attractions for all ages, from rolling dice for the parents to roller coasters for the kids, with a half dozen Cirque de Soleil productions, including the Beatles' Love, running 'round the clock. Back when, Vegas was an idea on the frontier. The state of Nevada seemed to allow legal gambling; therefore, might there rise in this lightly populated, largely ignored state—36th to be admitted to the union—a kind of tumbleweed Havana (which was an offshore haven that men such as Meyer Lansky knew and that was working very well)? Lansky and others placed their bets, and those gambles came home in spades. Sin City was a sensation, a place where men who had won the war could escape the suburbs for a weekend and get their sexy back. In the early years, Vegas looked bizarre from the skies, as we see here: a vast horizon of quite natural dryness, and in the foreground the neon-souled Sands, one of the anchors of what was quickly called "the strip."**

DON ENGLISH/LAS VEGAS NEWS BUREAU

THE BIRTH OF VEGAS, Part II. Elsewhere, there was a cold war, and therefore empty Nevada was useful in various ways. Sure, you could plop a floating crap game down in the pool at the Sands (left). Then too, in the vast desert outside of town you could experiment with your atomic bombs (below, a nuclear cloud as seen from downtown, and opposite, a cloud-hatted cutie smiling along with her friends in the military). It can be reasonably argued that Las Vegas in the 1950s was the strangest place on earth. In that era, gamblers would take a break from the tables and slots to venture outside for bomb-test parties, to be watched through sunglasses. There was a Miss Atomic Bomb beauty pageant. Then it would be back inside for an hour—seldom less, never more—of Sinatra or Don Rickles, Buddy Hackett, Shecky Greene, Louis Prima or the Mary Kaye Trio. The two-lane highway entering town from Los Angeles—now the cap-*S* Strip—became choked with casinos, as the Thunderbird, Flamingo and Sands were joined by dozens of others. Today, of course, there is a university in Las Vegas; native son Andre Agassi has built a charter school in an at-risk neighborhood; many hotels more closely resemble those of Disney World than they do the pioneer establishments of Sin City; golf courses and tennis courts are as backed up as the roulette tables. But back then: What a place!

LAS VEGAS NEWS BUREAU (2)

ALLAN GRANT/LIFE/THE PICTURE COLLECTION

a closed book that friends, lovers and wives felt they barely understood him. Sinatra's charisma, volatility and huge success in the 1950s made him a natural leader, with a group of followers and hangers-on who jumped at his every wish—and often flinched when his temper flared. Dean Martin wasn't one of Frank's followers—he followed nobody—but as their paths crossed more and more often (at Sinatra's initiation), he ceded the leadership role to him. "I don't think Dean was afraid of Sinatra, I think he just didn't want to get involved," says the comedian Shecky Greene, who worked frequently with both men and knew them well. "He didn't give a s---. Somebody had to be the don, so he let Sinatra be the don."

And in 1958, Sinatra was the don. He was vying head-to-head with Elvis Presley as America's leading recording artist, and his movie career, as star and producer, had rebounded so strongly that he was now able to call the shots with MGM, the same studio that had dropped him just a few years earlier. And for *Some Came Running,* the first movie in a three-picture deal with Metro, Frank insisted that Dean Martin be hired as his costar.

In the film, based on a novel by James Jones (who'd also written the book from which *From Here to Eternity* was adapted), Frank Sinatra played an ex-GI named Dave Hirsh who goes back to his Indiana hometown after *(continued on page 27)*

"SOME CAME RUNNING" was made in 1958 and brought together three of the six who would form the core of Rat Pack 2.0: Dean Martin (above, left), Shirley MacLaine (above and opposite) and Frank Sinatra (opposite, right). The relationships of these three superstars would be loyal, long-standing and just a little bit strange.

EVERETT

DEAN AND FRANK in the studio in 1958.

ALLAN GRANT/LIFE/THE PICTURE COLLECTION

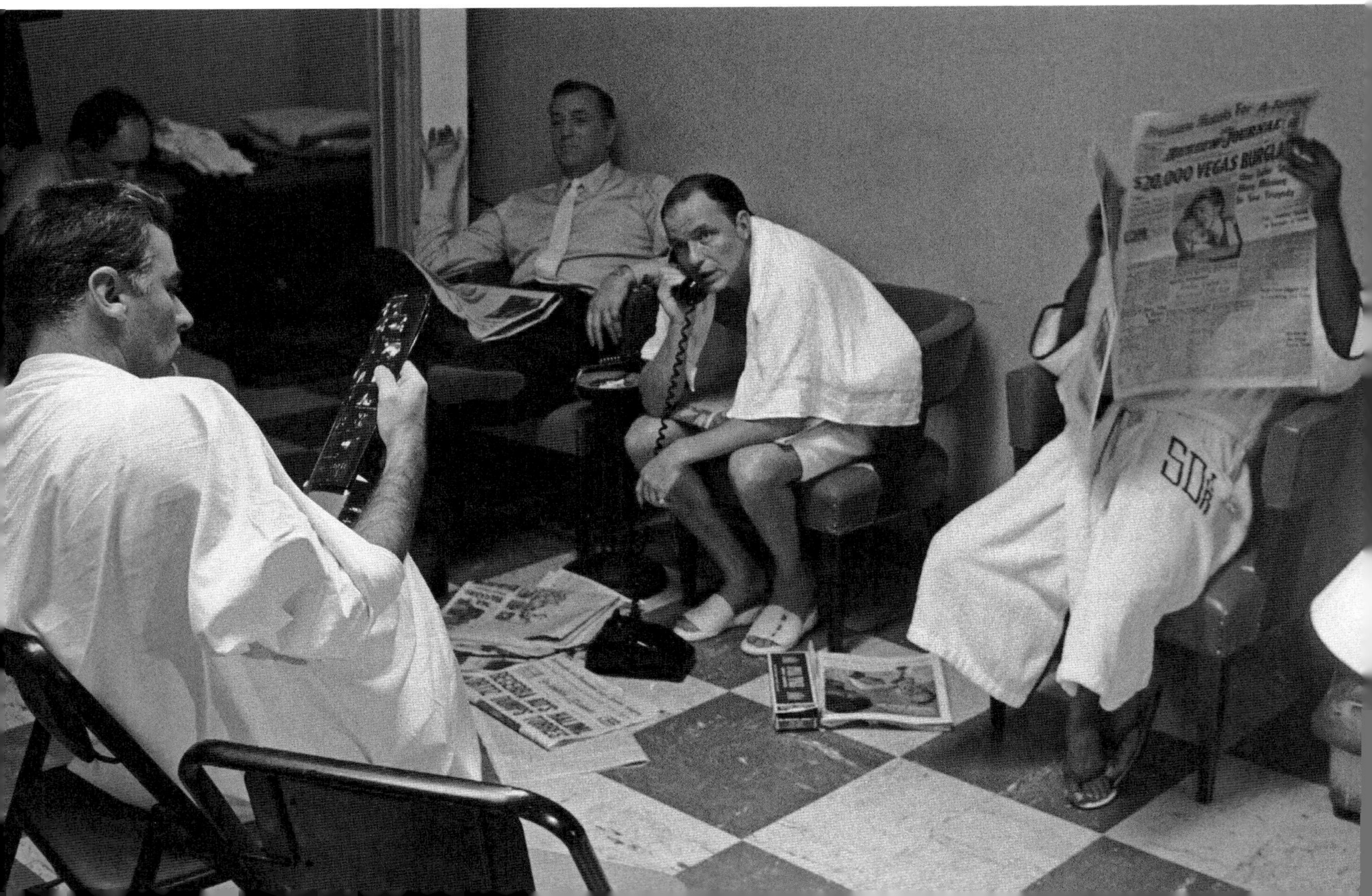
$20,000 VEGAS BURGLA

the war with the idea of becoming a writer. Martin played Bama Dillert, a deceptively easygoing southern gambler who becomes friendly with Hirsh. “Bringing his own background as a card dealer to the role of Bama, Martin conveys a sense of hidden danger, an exceedingly calm exterior masking the tough interior,” writes Tom Santopietro in *Sinatra in Hollywood.* Dean’s acting in the picture deeply impressed the 24-year-old Shirley MacLaine, who, in a role that would win her an Oscar nomination (and whose casting in the movie Frank had insisted on), played Sinatra’s character’s floozy girlfriend. “Dean’s performance in *Some Came Running* was his best, I thought,” she writes in her memoir *My Lucky Stars.* “He was a lot like Bama, a loner with his own code of ethics who would never compromise, so maybe it wasn’t really a performance.”

Martin may have been a loner, but Sinatra liked having him around. Within six months, Frank would conduct a new album by Dean, *Sleep Warm* (the title was a Sinatra catchphrase), and the two men would appear together for the first time on the stage of the Sands, earning a rave review in *Variety.*

There was someone else Frank liked having around too: Chicago mob boss Sam “Momo” Giancana. Giancana, who’d worked his way up from Al Capone’s errand boy in the 1920s to kingpin of the Windy City’s rackets, had first met Sinatra in the early ’50s and had helped the singer when his career slumped. Nightclubs were a key part of American show business then, and the mob ran the clubs, a natural consequence of organized crime’s control of the liquor business during Prohibition. Giancana was in a position to get Frank Sinatra work when nobody else would give it to him,

ALLAN GRANT/LIFE/THE PICTURE COLLECTION

JOHN COOK/LAS VEGAS NEWS BUREAU

and Sinatra was grateful: He gave the mobster a star-sapphire friendship ring in thanks.

Giancana had a certain fascination with show business, and he liked Frank Sinatra and even admired his talent. But ultimately he was a killer, a cold pragmatist who viewed entertainers as chips in a game, commodities to be manipulated. Sinatra, on the other hand, admired Sam Giancana as a man of power: He sought the gangster out as a friend, and strove to please him. Dean Martin, remote and practical, saw Giancana for what he was, understood his power and was accommodating and cordial—when necessary. Finally, though, Martin was always his own man.

During the three weeks of location shooting for *Some Came Running* in the hamlet of Madison, Indiana, in August and September of 1958, Sam Giancana was a frequent visitor to the set, along with several of his minions. “I didn’t know who they were,” Shirley MacLaine recalled. “I only knew that the nightlife of poker, jokes, pasta and booze went on until five a.m. Our calls were at six a.m.”

It was a new Rat Pack, in embryo.

THE SANDS WAS HOME. That’s the easiest way to think of it: The Sands was home. For a few years, the men lived here as much as they lived anywhere. In the photograph opposite, top, Martin is dealing blackjack, and in the bottom photo, Lawford, Sinatra and Davis chill outside the Sands steam room. They were royalty: They could be in charge or they could be customers, as they chose. The marquee above indicates how they were all often in residence, especially when *Ocean’s Eleven* was filming and then being released. One Packer might be headlining, the others might be mingling backstage—and then spilling forth.

BOB WILLOUGHBY/MPTVIMAGES

IN THE SUN
FRANK SINATRA
DEAN MARTIN
SAMMY DAVIS JR.
PETER LAWFORD
JOEY BISHOP

EVERETT

REAL WORLD? Well, was there any such thing in Las Vegas? From left, we have Richard Benedict, Clem Harvey, Norman Fell, Buddy Lester, Dean Martin, Henry Silva, Joey Bishop, Sammy Davis Jr., Peter Lawford and Frank Sinatra in 1960, making quite like a mob outside the Sands. But as it happens this exceedingly strange (and now historic) photograph, especially with the absolutely unique listing of all five core Rat Packers on the marquee in the background, was for the movie *Ocean's Eleven* and so can be seen as more fiction than fact. But what was fact, really, in that place at that time? What was day and what was night? From a LIFE article of the era: "It was six a.m. before the party got to Frank's suite. But the evening was not over because Frank hadn't said it was over. 'Everybody have a little more gasoline,' he ordered. Everybody did. They threw darts at a target on the wall. Frank was good at it. From the kitchen came a shout. A couple of guys were wrestling around. Frank went to see. Somebody got a raw egg broken on him. Then somebody else did. The sun was up at seven when Frank announced he was going to bed."

Frank Sinatra and Peter Lawford had become fast friends when both were contract stars at MGM in the mid-1940s. Sinatra was instantly drawn to the handsome young English expatriate, who could sing and dance and do comedy or drama with equal flair—and who, like Sinatra, loved to drink and chase women. Yet unlike Sinatra, who was a volcano of talent and ambition, Lawford was an underachiever, content to glide along and do whatever studio boss Louis B. Mayer asked him to. Maybe he could've been another Cary Grant, but for the moment, being Peter Lawford was working out just fine. Hedonistic and slightly cynical underneath his veneer of geniality, he was the perfect partner in crime for Frank Sinatra.

Until he committed the unforgivable offense. One night in late 1953, when Sinatra was down on his luck and Ava Gardner had one foot out the door, Lawford and his manager went out for a perfectly

LAWFORD AND DAVIS in Vegas, 1962

JOHN LOENGARD/LIFE/THE PICTURE COLLECTION

FRANK, WEARING an eye patch in solidarity with Sammy, yucks it up with Peter and Pat Lawford at Romanoff's in Hollywood in 1959.

MURRAY GARRETT/GETTY

THE MAN who would be President would also be Peter Lawford's avenue back into Sinatra's good graces and, thence, into the Rat Pack. Above, on November 15, 1958, Senator John F. Kennedy of Massachusetts is in Santa Monica, California, to serve as godfather to Peter and Pat's infant daughter, Victoria Francis, so named because she was born on November 4, which was a day of victory for Jack at the polls, and in honor of a family friend, Francis Sinatra. The baby was the Lawfords' third child. On the opposite page, top, Sinatra schmoozes with Senator Kennedy at a fund-raiser in L.A. on July 10, 1960—the eve of his selection as the Democratic presidential nominee, a goal that had been avidly sought by both men and that Sinatra and his mob associates had helped secure. Bottom: The following day, just before the party chooses its man, Sinatra is in attendance as the four top candidates for the nomination—Missouri senator Stuart Symington, Texas senator Lyndon Baines Johnson, Kennedy and twice-defeated presidential candidate Adlai E. Stevenson—make a show of allegiance.

innocent drink in Hollywood with Gardner and her sister. But then a gossip columnist had the manager and the sister airbrushed out of the picture, reporting that Peter Lawford had gone on a date with the still-married-to-Sinatra Ava Gardner. Frank, who had a hair-trigger temper at the best of times, and was now in his worst of times, went ballistic. Beyond ballistic—thermonuclear. He phoned Lawford at three a.m. and threatened to have his legs broken. Given Sinatra's acquaintances, the threat was not an idle one. Terrified, Lawford had his manager call Sinatra and explain what had really happened. Frank even believed Lawford—but, being Frank, refused to forgive him.

Fast-forward five years. In the interim, Peter—whose movie career had sputtered out after MGM dropped him—had made a spectacular marriage, to Patricia Kennedy, of the prominent Massachusetts political family. In 1958, Pat's older brother John, having risen to national fame at the 1956 Democratic National Convention, was actively running for President. One night, while Pat waited for Peter at a Hollywood dinner party (Lawford was working late on his new TV series, *The Thin Man*), Frank Sinatra—whom Pat Lawford, as a budding Hollywood hostess, had been trying to cultivate for years, only to be harshly rebuffed every time—appeared across the room. To her amazement, Sinatra turned his electric blues on her—the gaze that had melted thousands of female hearts—and made a beeline for her table. Sitting down next to her, he began to converse as though the two of them were old friends.

Then Peter Lawford showed up at the party and saw his wife sitting with Sinatra.

Everybody in the room knew the history of the falling out between the two men. Lawford hesitantly walked up to the table, whereupon Sinatra said to Pat Lawford: "You know, your old man and I aren't speaking."

The room fell silent. But then Sinatra smiled that miraculous smile, and there was relieved laughter all around. Frank Sinatra, who almost never uttered the words "I'm sorry," hadn't admitted to an error, but he had officially forgiven Peter Lawford—for one very pragmatic reason along with the emotional ones: Sinatra, a passionate Democrat, had become fascinated with Jack Kennedy and thought he had a real chance of becoming President. And he wanted to get close to him by whatever means possible.

And Peter Lawford had every reason to want to mend fences with the biggest star in show business. Accordingly, he laid out $10,000 of his and Pat's money—big money then—to buy a story idea he thought would interest Sinatra as a movie producer and actor.

A couple of years earlier, Lawford had run into an aspiring director named Gilbert L. Kay on the beach in Santa Monica, and Kay had told him about a movie idea: A group of World War II *(continued on page 36)*

DAVID SMITH/AP

BETTMANN/GETTY (2)

SINATRA LIT KENNEDY'S CIGARETTES and he would have carried his bags—something he would not have done for many other people in the world. "For a brief moment he was the biggest star in our lives," Sinatra said much later. "I loved him." If it seemed for a time that Frank and Jack represented a mutual admiration society, the facts were that, while Sinatra hero-worshipped Kennedy, Kennedy, as President, had little problem disassociating himself from the mob-linked singer when his brother, U.S. Attorney General Robert F. Kennedy, instructed him to do so. Needless to say this infuriated the short-fused entertainer, who had just finished the "Kennedy Wing" of his Palm Springs compound, dreaming it would be the Hyannis Port of the West. When JFK checked in at Bing Crosby's house up the road instead, a plaque was left behind to tarnish on the door of Sinatra's guest house: JOHN F. KENNEDY SLEPT HERE, NOVEMBER 6TH AND 7TH, 1960.

veterans, former commandos, join forces to rob five Las Vegas casinos simultaneously. It sounded like a great notion, but Kay wanted to direct the picture. Hollywood projects happen when powerful people make them happen, and at the time, Lawford and Kay were near the bottom of the food chain. Lawford passed. But now that he had mended fences with Frank Sinatra, he saw a way to get even further into the star's good graces. When Lawford told Sinatra about the idea, Frank smiled. He didn't just like it, he loved it.

Frank Sinatra and Sammy Davis Jr. also went way back—to 1941, when Sinatra was still singing with the Tommy Dorsey band and the 16-year-old Davis, a singing and dancing whirlwind starring in the Will Mastin Trio, first shook hands with his idol backstage at a theater in Detroit. Six years later, Sinatra—who was now singing on his own and, as both a passionate practitioner of racial tolerance and a canny stage-manager of his own shows, always wanted black acts to open for him—insisted the management hire the Mastin Trio, at five times their usual salary, when he played the Capitol Club in New York. A fast friendship was born between Frank and the diminutive Sammy, who in many ways was every bit as talented as the singer he adored.

With the Mastin Trio and then as a solo act in the early '50s, Davis frequently performed in Las Vegas, where his path often crossed with Sinatra's and their friendship deepened. Vegas was a remote outpost then, not far past the Old West days when cowboys and workers from the newly built Hoover Dam used to roll into town to get drunk, get laid and gamble away their salaries. "On Fremont Street," recalls Jerry Lewis, who performed at the Flamingo with Dean Martin beginning in the late 1940s, "they had a place to *tie your horse*!" Out along Route 91, the two-lane blacktop that would eventually become the Strip, there were wide stretches of desert between the dozen or so casinos, punctuated only by tumbleweed and rattlesnakes.

And being a cowboy town, Las Vegas was also a strictly segregated place. When Sammy Davis Jr. performed at the Frontier Hotel & Casino, he was not permitted to stay at the hotel or eat in the establishment's restaurants. After his show was over, he had to go back to a rooming house in the black district on the rundown west side of Vegas. It was this way at every casino on the Strip. Frank Sinatra hated this and vowed to do something about it as soon as he was able.

CBS/GETTY

CAMERA BUFF DAVIS takes note of the equipment before a 1955 appearance at home in Los Angeles on the popular interview show *Person to Person*, hosted from a New York studio by Edward R. Murrow. Murrow's guests in the 1950s included a who's who of the highest-ranking members of both famous Rat Packs: Humphrey Bogart, Lauren Bacall, Tony Curtis, Janet Leigh, Kirk Douglas, Frank Sinatra, Dean Martin, Sammy—not to mention Jack Kennedy.

But Davis would soon have troubles other than discrimination. On the night of November 19, 1954, as he was driving to Los Angeles from Las Vegas, he swerved to avoid hitting a car that was in the middle of the road preparing to turn around, and he collided with another vehicle. His head snapped forward into a conical ornament in the center of the steering wheel. The ornament struck Davis square in the left eye, nearly killing him and destroying the eye. As he lay in the hospital, he despaired of ever performing again. Many of Hollywood's biggest stars rallied to his side, including Sinatra, who insisted that Davis recuperate at his house in Palm Springs.

It was a strange thing: Before the accident, Sammy had been a star; afterward, his fame multiplied. Something about his vulnerability, something about Hollywood's love for him—even his new glass eye and his new conversion to Judaism: All of it took him over the top and made him a national personage. In 1956, a Broadway musical called *Mr. Wonderful*, crafted just to showcase his talents, was a big hit.

But even with all his bounce-back success and enormous gifts (he was also a brilliant impressionist), Davis lived in fealty to his close friend, older-brother surrogate and show-business godfather, Frank Sinatra. And friendship with Sinatra had strict rules. Frank picked up all checks. Frank gave you gifts; you did not give him gifts. (If you did give him a present, he would have to give you a bigger one soon thereafter.) If you hung out with him, you were in it for the long haul—hangout time began late at night, after the shows were over, and lasted until the sky began to lighten. No exceptions, no questions asked. Sinatra needed company, he demanded company, and you had to sit with him, listen to his stories about the old days with Dorsey, laugh at his jokes and be amusing company yourself—but not so amusing that you outshone the Chairman of the Board.

And most of all, you never crossed him. There were those big men (called the Necks, in recognition of their large collar sizes) around him, who threatened violence to anyone who stepped out of line. And then there was Sinatra's ferocious temper, which could be set off by the slightest infraction. Lawford had learned this lesson, to his sorrow. If you didn't like the way things went in Frank's circle, you either kept quiet

SAMMY VISITS FRANK on the set of *Some Came Running* in 1958, opposite. On this page, below, in July 1960, as Democrats gather in L.A. for their national convention, Adlai Stevenson poses for Davis as Judy Garland smiles. Bottom: On November 14, 1960, Sinatra, Davis and Lawford celebrate at the wedding of Davis to actress May Britt, which Sammy had delayed until after the election out of consideration for the Kennedy campaign.

BETTMANN/GETTY (2)

EVERETT

about it or left the circle. There was no middle ground, as Sammy Davis soon discovered.

In March 1959, having seen Sinatra behave badly once too many times, Davis spoke candidly—and as it turned out, indiscreetly—to a Chicago radio interviewer: "I love Frank and he was the kindest man in the world to me when I lost my eye in an auto accident and wanted to kill myself," he said. "But there are many things he does that there are no excuses for. Talent is not an excuse for bad manners—I don't care if you are the most talented person in the world. It does not give you the right to step on people and treat them rotten. This is what he does occasionally."

The "occasionally" didn't help. And it got even worse. When the interviewer asked Davis who the biggest singer in the country was, Sammy said it was he, himself, Sammy Davis Jr.

"Bigger than Frank?"

"Yeah."

This was very bad. Worst of all was that Sammy had dissed Frank in Chicago, home of Giancana and Sinatra's other mob pals. Word made its way quickly back to Sinatra, who had the predictable reaction. Code Red. DefCon One. Most importantly, he wrote Sammy out of the sketch.

It's just an expression, with broad metaphorical implications, yet in this case it was also literal. In the months since Frank had mended fences with Peter Lawford, he'd been developing *Never So Few,* a movie set in World War II Burma, as a starring vehicle for himself. The film was a coproduction between his production company and MGM, the studio that had dropped him in 1950. Now the power was in Sinatra's hands, and to flaunt it, he pressured Metro to sign their other reject, Lawford, to costar at a hugely inflated salary. Another power play had been to put his pal Sammy Davis into the picture. When an MGM producer objected, "Frank, there were no Negroes in the Burma theater [of operations]," Sinatra said, "Now there are."

And now there weren't. In the wake of Davis's Chicago debacle, Frank quickly had his old friend written out of the picture and the young Steve McQueen cast in his place.

"You wanna talk destroyed?" recalled Peter Lawford's manager Milt Ebbins. "Sammy Davis cried from morning to night. He came to see us when Peter was at the Copacabana, appearing with Jimmy Durante. He said, 'I can't get Frank on the phone. Can't you guys do something?' Peter told him, 'I talked to Frank, but he won't budge.' Sammy never did the picture, never got any money. He could have sued because he had a contract, but he didn't dare. You don't sue Frank Sinatra."

"Sammy was quite lucky," Lawford told a biographer. "Frank let him grovel for a while and then allowed him to apologize in public a few months later."

Davis never made it back into *Never So Few,* but he did get written into another new Sinatra movie project, that little thing about the Las Vegas casino heist. *(continued on page 44)*

BETTMANN/GETTY

ON JANUARY 27, 1961, comedian Jan Murray, Martin, Davis and Sinatra enjoy a smoke and a laugh backstage at Carnegie Hall during a benefit for civil rights leader Martin Luther King Jr.

NAT DALLINGER/CAMERA PRESS/REDUX

THERE WERE FEW or no rules when the Rat Pack took the stage, as here at the Cocoanut Grove in Los Angeles in 1960. At left is Sinatra, at right is Martin, and harmonizing is Bishop, but who has seized the microphone? Well, that would be Pack associate Eddie Fisher, who at the time enjoyed a reputation even more notorious than his friends', having left his wife and America's Sweetheart Debbie Reynolds for Elizabeth Taylor. Formerly a Goody Two-shoes (with a secret drug addiction and serious gambling problem; back in 1955 Fisher had enraged his bride, Reynolds, when he had left the honeymoon suite to join a poker game featuring Sinatra, Lawford and Davis), he had forfeited his television show in the Liz-over-Debbie scandal, which was much more outrageous—in a tabloid sense—than anything that can be imagined today. But nobody was too hot for the Pack, and a friend of Frank's was a friend for life, unless or until he or she crossed Frank, which Fisher did not. So, sure, Eddie: Come on up! Show the folks what you've got, and have a little gasoline on us. (Gas being fuel, or booze; we'll delve more deeply into Rat Pack lingo shortly.) Rat Pack performances weren't exactly "all comers," but they were ragged affairs with regular shout-outs to pals in the audience. There was some singing but a lot of horseplay, and insult humor was at a premium. It can only be imagined how many "How's Debbie doing?" jokes were tossed across the stage at the Grove this night.

And then there was Joey.

Joey Bishop, né Joseph Abraham Gottlieb, was a nervous, obscure nightclub comic who could barely get arrested when he had the life-changing good fortune of being spotted by Frank Sinatra in New York in the early '50s. Sinatra liked Bishop's deadpan, pessimistic style, the fact that he almost never smiled onstage: He was like a Jewish Buster Keaton. Soon Bishop was opening for Sinatra at New York–area clubs like the Copacabana and the Riviera—and then, in 1956, at Frank's Las Vegas home base, the Sands. (In 1953, the casino's eastern owners, including mobster Joseph "Doc" Stacher, had allowed Sinatra to purchase two points in the establishment, in recognition of the high-rolling crowd his performances there always drew.)

But as Frank's career skyrocketed through the '50s, Bishop's wobbled along, never quite taking off. To the general public Joey was an acquired taste; he was tagged with that most ambivalent label, a "comedian's comedian." And true to form, show-business crowds loved him: At a Friar's roast of Dean Martin in 1958, after celebrity upon celebrity got up and declared how thrilled they were to be there, Bishop finally came to the podium and stared bleakly out at the star-studded crowd for a long moment. "I was *told* to come here," he said at last. The audience roared—including Frank, who in all likelihood was the one who'd done the telling.

Now Sinatra had another job in mind for Joey, and a few more of his pals as well.

The Vegas movie, now called *Ocean's Eleven,* had a plot that sounded great on paper: 11 former army buddies band together to rob five Vegas casinos—the Sands, the Flamingo, the Sahara, the Desert Inn and the Riviera—simultaneously, at the stroke of midnight on New Year's Eve. In fact, the script (which had gone through a half-dozen writers) was a hodgepodge of

BOB WILLOUGHBY/MPTVIMAGES

AN EARLY NEWS feature on *Ocean's Eleven* from the *New York Times* reported that after Sinatra and Lawford purchased the screenplay, neither intended to appear on camera. Plans changed and Sinatra took the lead on screen, with Lawford playing one of the crew. Sinatra is seen here during production of the film.

CASHIE
HOTEL SAHARA
HOTEL SAHARA

plot mechanics, but the film's plot was secondary in any case: It was ultimately a character-driven piece. And Frank Sinatra knew plenty of characters.

Frank would, of course, play the lead, Danny Ocean, the former sergeant in the 82nd Airborne Division who masterminded the heist and assembled the crew. Dean Martin would play Sam Harmon, a lounge singer who was ambivalent about taking part in the caper. Peter Lawford was to play Jimmy Foster, a playboy eager to get out from under the thumb of his rich mother. Sammy Davis Jr. was cast as Josh Howard, a former baseball player who'd lost an eye in the war and now drove a garbage truck in Las Vegas.

The movie had strands of reality—some clear, some strange—woven in. It was no stretch for Sinatra to play the smooth kingpin of a group of men: Ever since he'd started out as a singer, he'd gone around with a coterie of friends, acquaintances, gofers, hangers-on and tough guys—these days, it would be called a posse; then, it was known as the Varsity. Dean was essentially playing himself: He had begun his career singing in lounges, and truly was reluctant about joining any sort of group. Lawford's part—that of a feckless, sponging playboy—was painfully close to the bone. And was Sammy made to play a garbage man as some kind of punishment for his sins against Frank in the Chicago radio interview?

The strangest casting of all was Joey's: His character, Mushy O'Connors, was supposed to be an ex-boxer, though it was difficult to imagine the slight, dyspeptic comic as any kind of boxer, ex or otherwise.

Ocean's Eleven began shooting on location in Las Vegas in January 1960. And from the moment the cast showed up in town, through the film's premiere that August, and ever after, none of the leading players, or Vegas itself for that matter, would be the same.

HULTON/GETTY

IT WAS ALL happening simultaneously—the Rat Pack; *Ocean's Eleven*; the whole daily scene, real and imagined, at the Sands—and that's part of the reason why the history is often misunderstood. Some work did get done; the filmed results are evidence. Here, in 1960, the Russian-born director Lewis Milestone instructs Martin, Bishop and Davis on what is expected of them as members of Danny Ocean's gang. Whether Sinatra had yet awoken this day is uncertain.

"Cmdr. and Mrs. Orville W. Dryer of Point Mugu just returned from a week's stay in that neon never-never land that is Vegas. They were on hand opening night to view a nightclub act to end them all—'modestly' referred to by its stars as the summit meeting, starring Frank Sinatra, Dean Martin, Sammy Davis Jr., Peter Lawford, plus a quiet, deadpan comic named Joey Bishop, all at the Sands Hotel."

—*Oxnard* [CA] *Press-Courier*, January 29, 1960

Three weeks, from January 20 to mid-February 1960, was really all the time it lasted. Everything afterward was an echo, a kind of parody—though parody was what it was kind of all about in the first place.

Wasn't it?

The point is, there *was* no Rat Pack in the first place. No plan, no script, no starting pistol. Nobody ever preconceived the idea of rolling out these five guys and their bar cart on the stage of the Sands' Copa Room that January, as shooting for *Ocean's Eleven* began. This gang wouldn't even be called the Rat Pack until much later, and Sinatra always hated the name anyway—the word *rat* having negative connotations where he came from. "The Clan" would be tried out briefly, but Sammy Davis didn't like the sound of that too much. Finally, in tribute to the planned summit conference between President Eisenhower and Soviet Premier Nikita Khrushchev coming that May, someone—it might've been Sands manager and entertainment director Jack Entratter—decided to call the more or less spontaneous shows featuring Sinatra, Martin, Davis, Lawford and Bishop on the Copa Room's stage the Summit. "You come to my summit and I'll come to yours," Entratter wired the five entertainers late that January, signing the telegram "Khrushchev."

The Summit. A big, ponderous, vaguely hollow name for a couple hours' goofing around onstage. Goofing around by stars like these was, surprisingly, a fairly shocking thing in the small, tightly controlled, homogeneous town that was Las Vegas in 1960.

Anyone who's been to Vegas in the past decade or two, or even just seen *The Hangover*—anyone who has been fascinated or repelled by the pulsating mega-colossal electric ultra-corporate glass-tower light show that is Las Vegas today—will have to make a mental adjustment to imagine the nascent Vegas of that distant time, a small place with a downtown consisting of a few honky-tonk, neon-lit blocks along Fremont Street and, out along the Strip, just those mere dozen or so casinos with lots of desert in between; a place where the tallest building was nine stories high, and where, as Shecky Greene recalls, "everybody knew each other; everybody took care of each other." It was a time when the Mob controlled what went on in the casinos, and what went on outside was controlled by a kind of Old West justice—then and now, Vegas has had an actual sheriff (in 1960, it was Butch Leypoldt; after him came the legendary Ralph Lamb), and the sheriffs have been famously tough and incorruptible. It was a time, older residents recall wistfully, when you could leave your doors unlocked.

It was also a time when gambling reigned supreme, and entertainers were the tail of the dog: Entertainment was what drew the gamblers to town. Entertainers—even Frank Sinatra—were employees and, even in Sinatra's case, did what they were told. They came, they sang or told jokes, for two shows a night, 60 minutes each—not a minute more; the audience had to get back to gambling or the house would lose money. The cover charge for Sinatra's

A TRUE RARITY: A color portrait of the famous Pack in the famous place, everyone in attendance and looking chipper, lined up left to right in accordance with their billing on the marquee (and also in accordance with their relative standing in the group, despite the fact that Sammy, his name in red, seems to be headlining the evening's shows). What the Pack was up to was so loose and crazy, there was no thought given that a photo record of events might be invaluable more than a half century on.

FLOYD MCCARTY/MPTVIMAGES

Sands
A PLACE
IN THE SUN
FRANK SINATRA
DEAN MARTIN
SAMMY DAVIS JR.
PETER LAWFORD
JOEY BISHOP
IN THE LOUNGE

shows in the Copa Room in that era was $6.50—the equivalent of about $50 today, but still a relative pittance. And the entertainers were richly paid for their efforts (and many of them gambled away their salary before they left town). Then they'd cycle along to their jobs making records or movies or performing at clubs in other cities.

Ocean's Eleven changed all that.

But things didn't change all at once. Though Sinatra, Martin, Davis, Lawford and Bishop were in town to act in the movie (and were staying at the Sands), only Frank, Dean and Sammy were scheduled to headline at the Copa Room—individually, on successive nights. As Ed Walters, who began working as a pit boss at the Sands in 1959, recalls, "Frank opened the first night and all went well. Dean did the second night and did both shows." Then, on the third night, Sammy Davis Jr. was running long. A no-no.

"Frank came onstage, did some talking with Sammy and ended the show," Walters says. "He said, 'He's got to go to bed—we're doing a movie all day. Sammy, say goodnight.' Sammy says goodnight. Frank takes him by the hand and tells the crowd, 'I've got to get him to bed.' They both walk off to a big round of applause."

One headliner breaking into another headliner's show was highly unusual. But the next night, something even more remarkable occurred. "Frank is doing his show," Ed Walters remembers, "and out walks Dean and tells everyone *Frank* has to go to bed. The audience is shocked at first. Remember, this is Sinatra in the Copa Room in full tux, doing his usual very professional job. Frank would start a song and halfway through it, Dean would cut in—'Frank, that's enough. Frank, that song's too long—sing something shorter.'

"The crowd doesn't know if Dean is serious or not, if Dean is drunk or not. Dean did drink a lot at the

BOB WILLOUGHBY/MPTVIMAGES

THE PACK PERFORMS at the Sands, and these are of course Martin, Davis, Lawford, Sinatra, and Bishop, with Buddy Lester between Frank and Joey. Lester made his film debut in 1959's *The Gene Krupa Story* before he shared the screen with Sinatra and company in *Ocean's Eleven* and *Sergeants 3*. The actor went on to appear in Jerry Lewis's *Nutty Professor* and the 1970's crime television show *Starsky and Hutch*.

time. I know that this stuff would [later] become legend, but at the time it was a shocking thing to see."

What Martin was doing to Sinatra was the very thing Jerry Lewis had done to Dean Martin in 1946: interrupt a straight act with horseplay, unnerving the audience (and the performer) at first, but ultimately thrilling them. Everyone got to feel as if they were in on the joke; everyone could feel vicariously naughty. And Sinatra, by going along with the routine (and he seemed to have been truly startled by Martin at first), could feel vicariously funny. The laughs—the kind he could never get with his own jokes or asides—felt intoxicating to him.

"The audience just loved it and broke out in spontaneous applause," Walters says. "That show ended with the audience going out and raving about what they saw. Everyone in the casino talked about it—Dean and Frank were funny together! By the end of the first week, it was almost certain that at every show, no matter who was doing his show that night, Frank, Dean and Sammy would [all] be onstage [together]. The fooling around became the talk of the Strip and then the city, and then it spread to L.A. and New York. People were flying in from all over. Frank's friends all wanted to be there. Kirk Douglas, Cary Grant, Roz Russell,

BOB WILLOUGHBY/MPTVIMAGES

SINATRA NEVER LACKED for female companionship, and this was particularly true during his Rat Pack years after Ava Gardner had left him and then it ultimately didn't work out with Lauren Bacall. How many Copa Girls there might have been is lost to history, but among actresses he was linked with publicly in these years were Natalie Wood and, seen here in 1959, Juliet Prowse.

Gregory Peck and all his buddies came in and saw a show or two and went home raving about it."

The rumors were flying all over town, Ed Walters recalls: "'Dean was drunk and stopped Frank from singing!'

"'Frank and Dean were so drunk they couldn't remember the words, so they yelled at each other!'

"'You can't believe it—Sinatra was interrupted right in the middle of [singing] by Dean Martin and Sammy Davis, who told Sinatra to stand aside while they showed him how to do his act!'"

The word spread, and the stars, and the public, kept flocking to the Sands. Attention begat more attention. "Every night there was some important or well-known person at the shows," Walters says. "Marilyn Monroe, Cary Grant, Gregory Peck. If they were introduced during the show, and they all were, it made news. The press ate it up. They hadn't seen so many stars in one place in some time."

At one point in early February, the Sands had 18,000 reservation requests for its 200 rooms. Soon Peter Lawford and Joey Bishop were joining in, too. Lawford, who had sung and danced very creditably in MGM musicals, rolled out his old skills, and audiences were glad to see him. And Jack Entratter, who had honed his impresario skills back at the Copacabana, and was behind the scenes at the Copa Room, stage-managing this new whatever-it-was, had a very special role in mind for Bishop.

Entratter was delighted at the comedy chaos that was unfolding nightly and turning the Sands into the center of the entertainment universe—but he never forgot what the casino's main business was. Thus he assigned Joey Bishop to perform the critical function of emcee. It was Joey's job to control the onstage bedlam by introducing the act and then, after not too much more than an hour, making sure it got off in time for the gamblers to get back to gambling. But gradually, with Dean's help and Frank's blessing, Bishop, the straightest of straight men, also became part of the act. In the midst of all the nonsense, one long-suffering stare could go a long way.

"Frank Sinatra, Dean Martin, Sammy Davis Jr., Joey Bishop and Peter Lawford were supposed to take turns entertaining in the Copa room but save for one night when Dean was ill, they've all been on for two shows, and the performances get crazier each time. They had a cake throwing contest the night of Joey Bishop's birthday [February 3]. He saw it coming but Frank and Dean didn't and got it in the face and chest . . ."

—Hedda Hopper's syndicated column of February 11, 1960

And it *was* nonsense, mostly. What's usually said about the comedy that took place during those three weeks at the Sands is that you had to be there. What audiotaped and filmed records show students of the Rat Pack is that most of the humor was Neanderthal, if not antediluvian, at least by 21st-century standards. Lots of drinking jokes, mostly by Dean (after the initial ovation: "How long I been on?"). Lots of ethnic jokes, chiefly at Sammy's expense (Frank, from offstage: "Keep smiling so they can see you, Smokey"; and the famous—and oft reused—bit where Dean picked Sammy up bodily and perked up, "I'd like to thank the NAACP for this award"), but even one or two at Sinatra's (Joey: "Stop singing and tell people about all the good work the Mafia's doing").

Not everyone was charmed. "I thought it was plain, unadulterated s---," says Shecky Greene, who knew all the participants well and attended one of the shows. He shakes his head. "Calling [Sammy] 'Smokey' and 'Blackie'—I was offended."

But to the paying customers—say, the Orville Dryers of Point Mugu, California—it was all new, and profoundly startling. It was startling to see grown men in tuxedos—*famous* grown men in tuxedos—behaving this way, and no doubt the Dryers told their friends about it (whispering the naughty bits), and the legend began to grow. *(continued on page 62)*

BOB WILLOUGHBY/MPTVIMAGES (2)

LAWFORD, MARTIN, Bishop—taking a pie—Sinatra, Davis, and Buddy Lester in 1960.

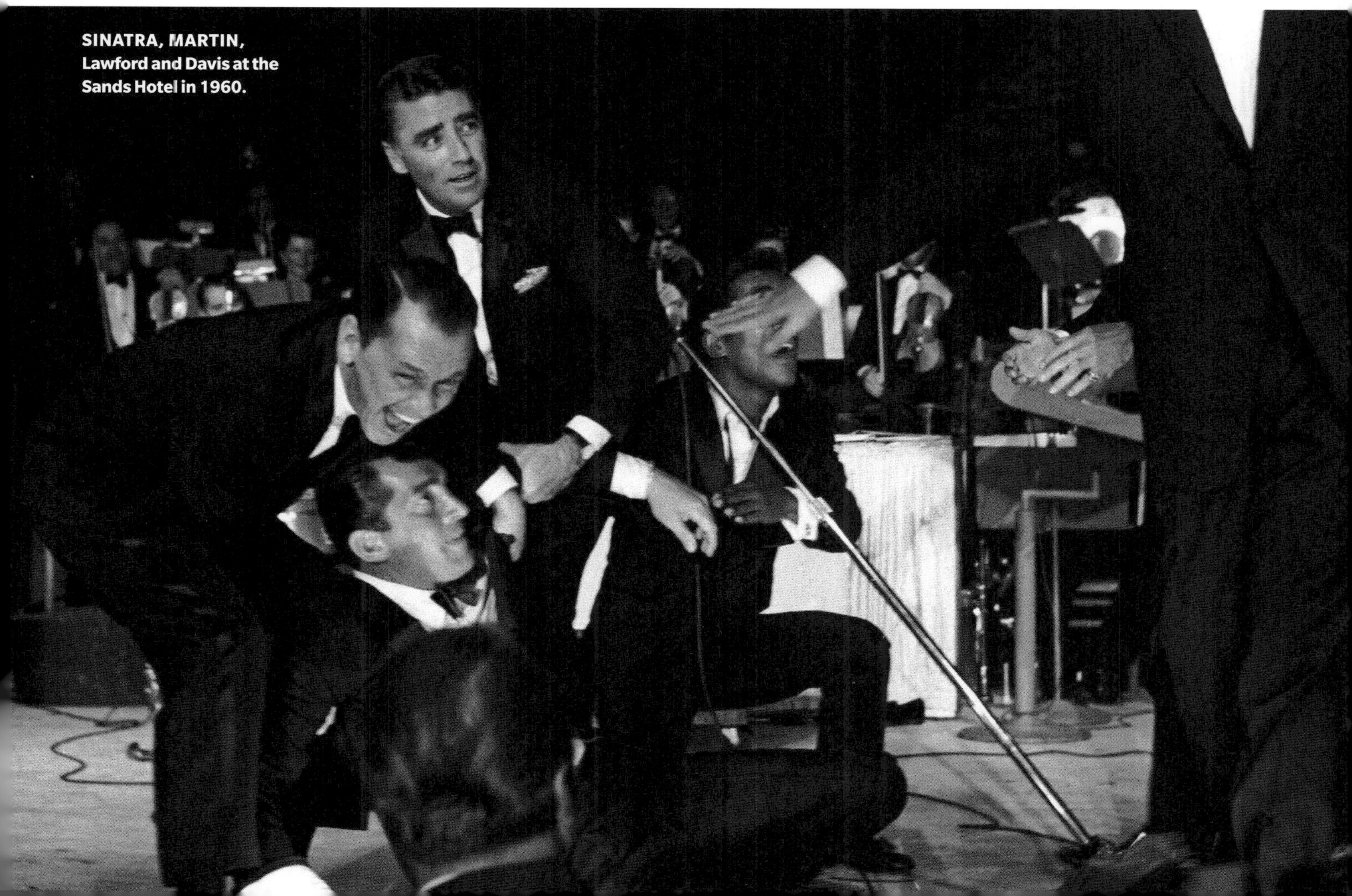

SINATRA, MARTIN, Lawford and Davis at the Sands Hotel in 1960.

JOHN DOMINIS/LIFE/THE PICTURE COLLECTION

WHOOPS! We said just pages ago that photographers weren't really paying close attention and the historical record is therefore scattered. That's not precisely true, thank goodness. Sinatra, icon above icons, was, in the earliest 1960s, approaching in age the big five-0, and at least two national magazines took note: *Esquire* and LIFE. *Esquire* sent the estimable Gay Talese out West and that resulted in the classic New Journalism profile "Frank Sinatra Has a Cold." LIFE put star staff photographer John Dominis on the case, and that resulted in a cover story that was the visual equivalent of Talese's rich rendering. Dominis recalls today that he hovered for the longest time, not even raising his camera, and then one day Sinatra—a photo buff himself, as was Sammy Davis Jr. (Sinatra would subsequently shoot an Ali-Frazier title bout for LIFE from a ringside seat in Madison Square Garden)—invited him along, saying basically, "Shoot away!" Dominis did, making 10,000 images in the next several weeks, and those pictures today constitute perhaps the liveliest and most intimate document of the Rat Pack milieu in all its outrageousness. In this quite obviously behind-the-scenes picture, Frank is horsing around with Jilly Rizzo, his forever friend and bodyguard (and also a saloon-keeper in the New York City joint Sinatra helped set up for him), while Ed Pucci, a 300-pound former football player who is also a *paisan* and aide-de-camp, raids the fridge.

WELL, THEY WERE DRUNK, weren't they? Certainly they were, especially the Leader. "I spill more than he drinks," said Sinatra correctly about Dean Martin, adding an eternal Rat Pack catchphrase: "That's an actuality." The cart they pushed onstage at the Sands bore the motto: DON'T THINK, DRIMK. Challenged by his doctor in this period, Sinatra admitted to three dozen drinks a day. The doctor, horrified, asked how he felt in the morning. "I don't know," said Sinatra. "I'm never up in the morning. And I'm not sure you're the doctor for me." The booze was a problem, however, and Sinatra knew it. Once, when his voice just wasn't there and he had to sing on TV, he was in the corner muttering, "Drink, drink, drink. Smoke, smoke, smoke. Schmuck, schmuck, schmuck." But he also said, many a time (and probably when these pictures were made for LIFE by John Dominis): "You die your way, I'll die mine." On this page, at top, he is closeted with a Pack associate in very good standing, comedian Joe E. Louis. Some few folks, like Louis, Dean Martin and the dour Joey Bishop, could crack him up just by saying something—anything. Sinatra loved having them around. In the photo at right, he falls off the chair in hilarity after Louis tells him a joke (perhaps the Louis staple: "You're not drunk if you can lie on the floor without holding on"). In the sequence on the opposite page, Sinatra loses a bet with the bare- and barrel-chested Ed Pucci that he can extract the tablecloth without disturbing the china. A gay time was had by all.

JOHN DOMINIS/LIFE/THE PICTURE COLLECTION (5)

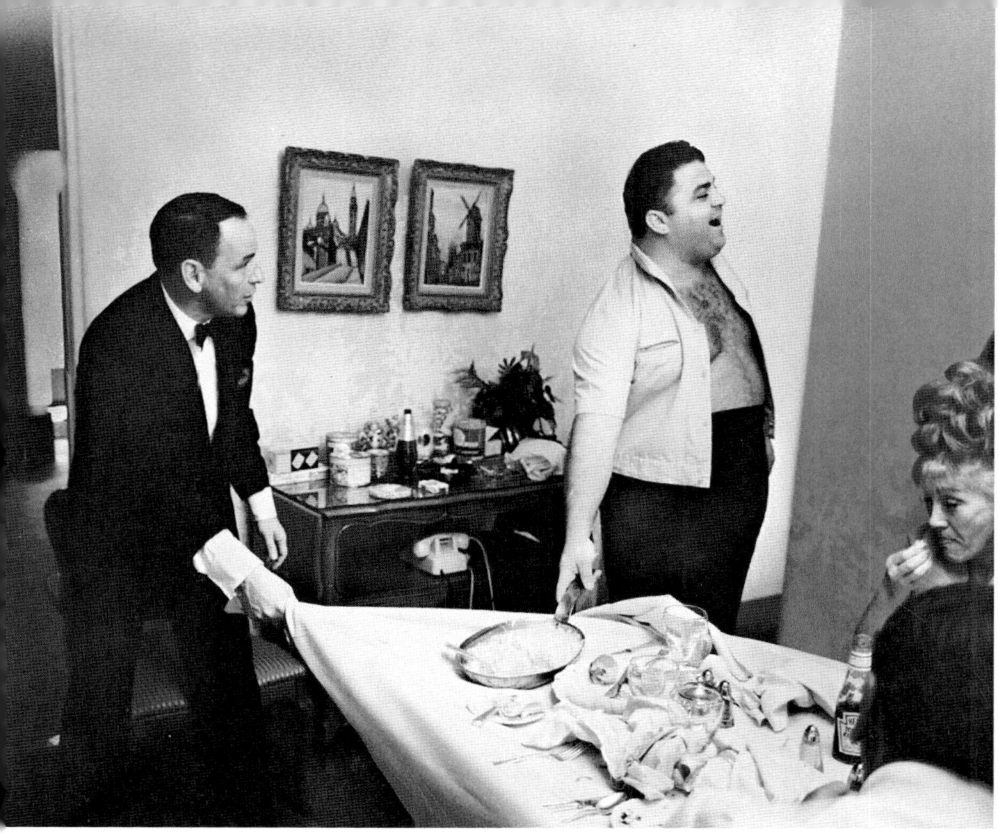

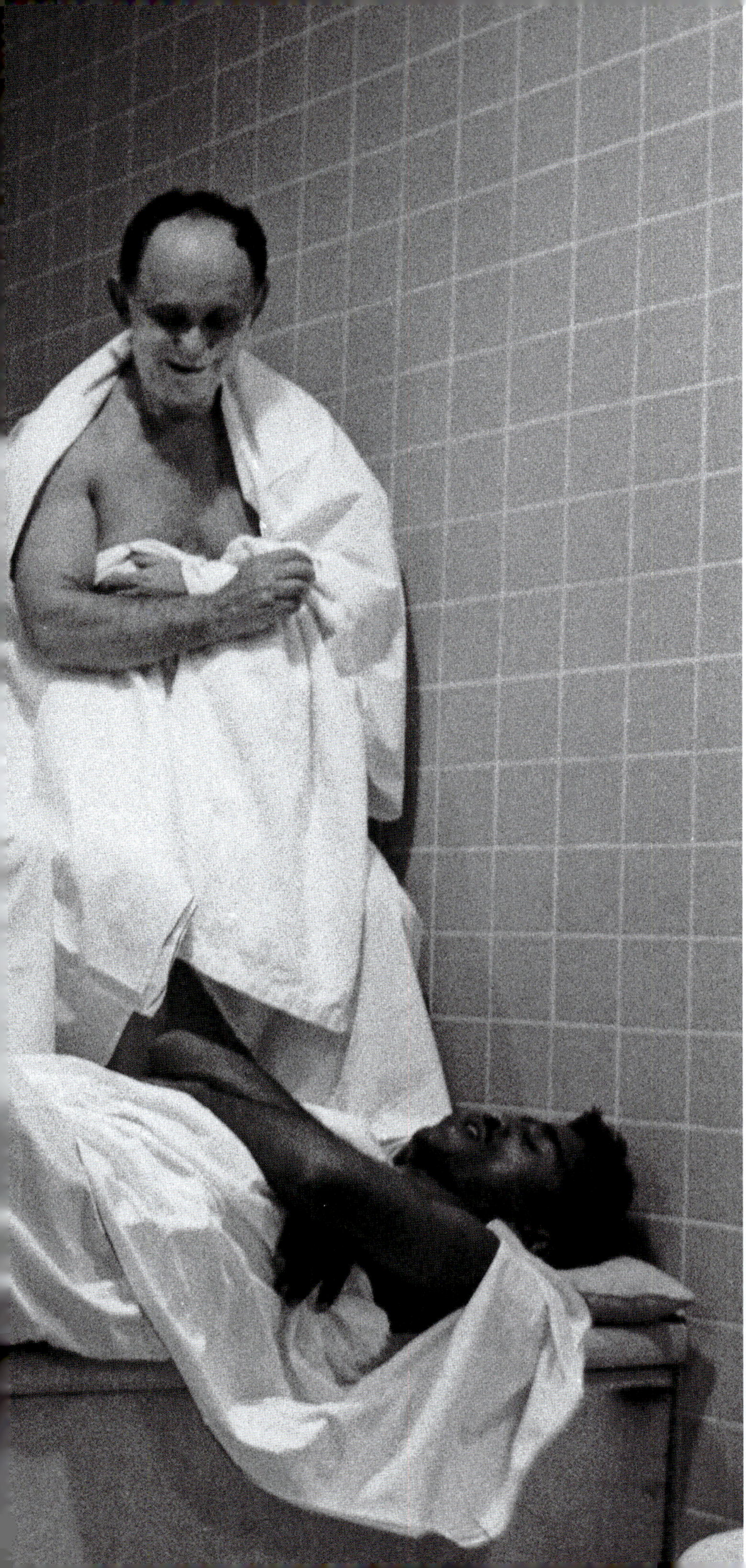

BOB WILLOUGHBY/MPTVIMAGES

THE PACK would never repent, but sometimes the Pack had to pay the piper. Here are, from left, Lawford, Sinatra, Beverly Hills banker Al Hart and Davis, supine (but happy to even be present in a usually segregated space), owning up for last night—whatever last night might have entailed—at the Sands. It's interesting and informative: Dean Martin and Joey Bishop are missing. Dino was surely on the putting green of the 10th hole at this moment, and Joey was enjoying a nice breakfast of eggs, toast and fruit juice; they were the ones who could and did resist the five a.m. last round. The rest of the Rat Pack at the Sands, and their friends, would not and could not and did not resist. From afar, you wondered what was really going on up there on the hotel's top floor, the floor no one could reach unless invited by the Leader. The answer: plenty. The Pack's regular gas, Jack Daniel's, had been joined by a superpremium, Chivas, and Sinatra would drive till dawn on either or both. The desert was a very wet place with the Pack in town. And as for the ladies, they were indeed allowed on the top floor—in quantity. "Frank wasn't a womanizer," said Tony Curtis, who was there. "He was womanized." And after all that booze and exercise: You had to sweat it out. As best you could.

During the day, they made the movie. Sort of. "The earliest call was for 5:30 p.m., and no actor had to be on the set for more than three hours," writes Shawn Levy, in *Rat Pack Confidential.* "On the first day of the Summit, January 20, there was no filming done at all. Thereafter, [director Lewis] Milestone usually got one Rat Packer at a time, occasionally two, having the whole quintet at his disposal only once—to film the closing credits on a workday cut short by high winds." Only Sammy, Peter and Joey ever worked in the morning—except for one time when Frank showed up at five a.m. for two hours of work; and then, probably, finally hit the sack.

How could, and why would, a movie be made under such circumstances? Because Frank Sinatra, the producer and star of *Ocean's Eleven,* was calling the shots, that's why. And, as Tom Santopietro writes, "Frank looked upon the film, in essence, as a very well-paid vacation. He did not invest any of his artistry or passion in it, but rather viewed it as a means to make money and have fun with his friends."

The distinguished 65-year-old Milestone, who had won an Oscar in 1930 for *All Quiet on the Western Front,* did the best he could under the circumstances, but "certainly knew exactly who held the power on the set," Santopietro notes. "Sinatra . . . stood right next to him behind the camera whenever his presence was not required for the scene being shot."

Did Sinatra also hold the power over the other four principals? In a famous Vegas story, the actor Norman Fell, a costar in *Ocean's Eleven,* is said to have awakened one morning—it must have been very late in the morning—and looked out his hotel window to see Dean and Sammy and Peter Lawford running past the pool. Fell stuck his head out and yelled, "Hey, where are you guys going?" And Sammy said, "Frank's up!"

It's a cute story; add it to the legend. The camaraderie onstage led the outside world to jump to conclusions. "Some eastern press, mainly one woman who had a column, put it out as 'Frank Sinatra and his pack of regulars are up all night drinking and partying in Las Vegas,'" Ed Walters says. "That wasn't exactly the correct scene as I saw it."

Was Sinatra the kingpin of the quintet? Without a doubt. "It's Frank's world, we just live in it," Dean Martin is supposed to have said; he may even have actually said it. All four of Sinatra's partners in the Summit were proud to call him a friend; they readily acknowledged him as the most powerful man in show business. But the reality was thornier. Dean Martin had huge admiration for Frank Sinatra as a singer, and loved him as a friend. But Sinatra's version of friendship demanded fealty, and Martin kowtowed to no one. He went his own way, and if things ever became confrontational, his way was to vanish.

Though Sammy Davis Jr. had some talents that Frank Sinatra could only dream of, and was nearly his equal in stardom, his relationship with Sinatra was uneasily sycophantic. The sight of him onstage during the Summit performances, bent over and grimacing with seemingly uncontrollable laughter as Sinatra clumsily mocked him, is painful. But like Peter Lawford, Davis knew all too well what could happen when you got on Frank's bad side.

As for Lawford, he held a certain amount of reflected power in 1960 because his wife's brother was well on the way to being elected President (Sinatra's nickname for him during that period: "Brother-in-Lawford"). But Peter was widely seen as being a toady and errand boy. "He was hanging around Frank all the time," Walters remembers. "It was Sinatra being the boss and Lawford being the employee. One of [Don] Rickles's great jokes was, 'Peter, you can laugh. Frank says it's okay.' Because we all knew Lawford didn't do *anything* without Frank's okay. Frank didn't treat him like a friend."

And Joey Bishop was never going to be one of Sinatra's drinking buddies—the only kind of buddy Sinatra had—for one important reason: He didn't drink. "We've worked together many times, and I enjoy it, but we don't socialize afterwards," Bishop admitted.

The socializing afterwards was one of the most important things in Sinatra's *(continued on page 68)*

REALITY BLURRED when the screenplay that Lawford (bare-chested) brought to Sinatra (in a fabulous fuzzy sweater) was filmed in and around the Sands. This scene might as well have been real—as real as "real" was, anyway, in Vegas—but in fact this is a still from the film. The fact that *Ocean's Eleven,* a medium movie, has gone on to be an enduring and oft-remade cultural artifact is as bizarre as the fact that Rat Pack books are still being written and published a half century after that fact (if there even was, in fact, any fact).

WARNER BROTHERS/ENTERTAINMENT PICTURES/ZUMA

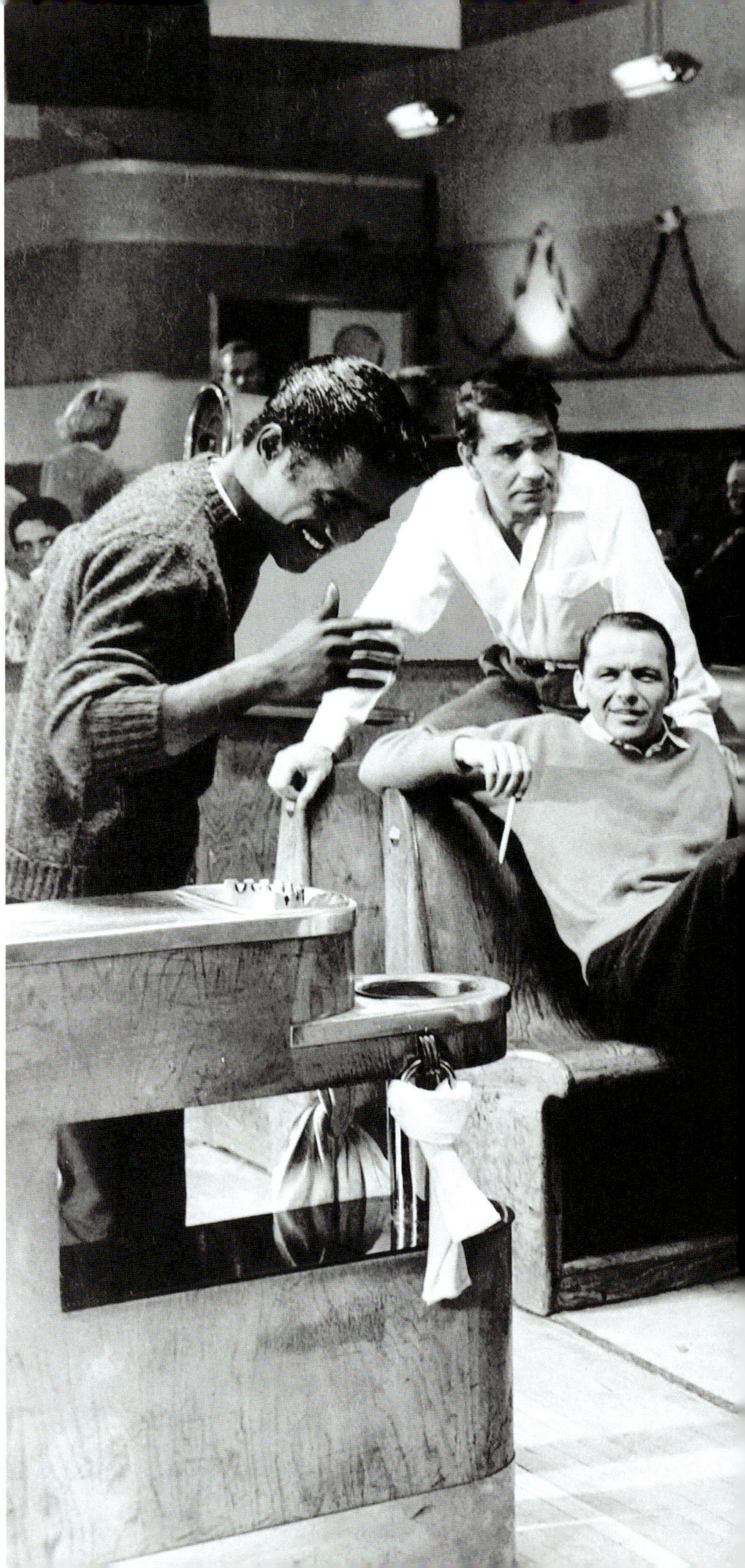

WARNER BROTHERS/UPPA/PHOTOSHOT

SINATRA SAW FROM THE FIRST that *Ocean's Eleven* was not only right for him, it fit his Pack—whatever pack that was as the 1950s ceded to the '60s and Frankie Boy found himself in charge of not only Vegas and an entourage but the wider entertainment world. He certainly had enough pals and gals in close proximity to effortlessly fill the roles. The five-pack was in the movie, of course, and so were Richard Conte, Cesar Romero, Henry Silva, Akim Tamiroff, Red Skelton, Norman Fell, Ilka Chase, Buddy Lester and on and on. In this photograph, Sammy is laughing, Sinatra is presiding, Dino is in the balcony, Peter is intent—leaning on his elbows—and Joey is either behind Peter or he's momentarily absent. Peter's beverage seems to be coffee, so this is during the filming of the movie, not later in the day when this crew was prowling (or presiding in) the casino. Sinatra and filmdom were funny: He was sometimes fine, but he—"the singer"—was always at a remove or even at odds. He hated his costar in *Guys and Dolls,* Marlon Brando, calling him "the most overrated actor in the world." Brando rejoined: "When he dies and goes to heaven, the first thing he'll do will be to find God and yell at him for making him bald."

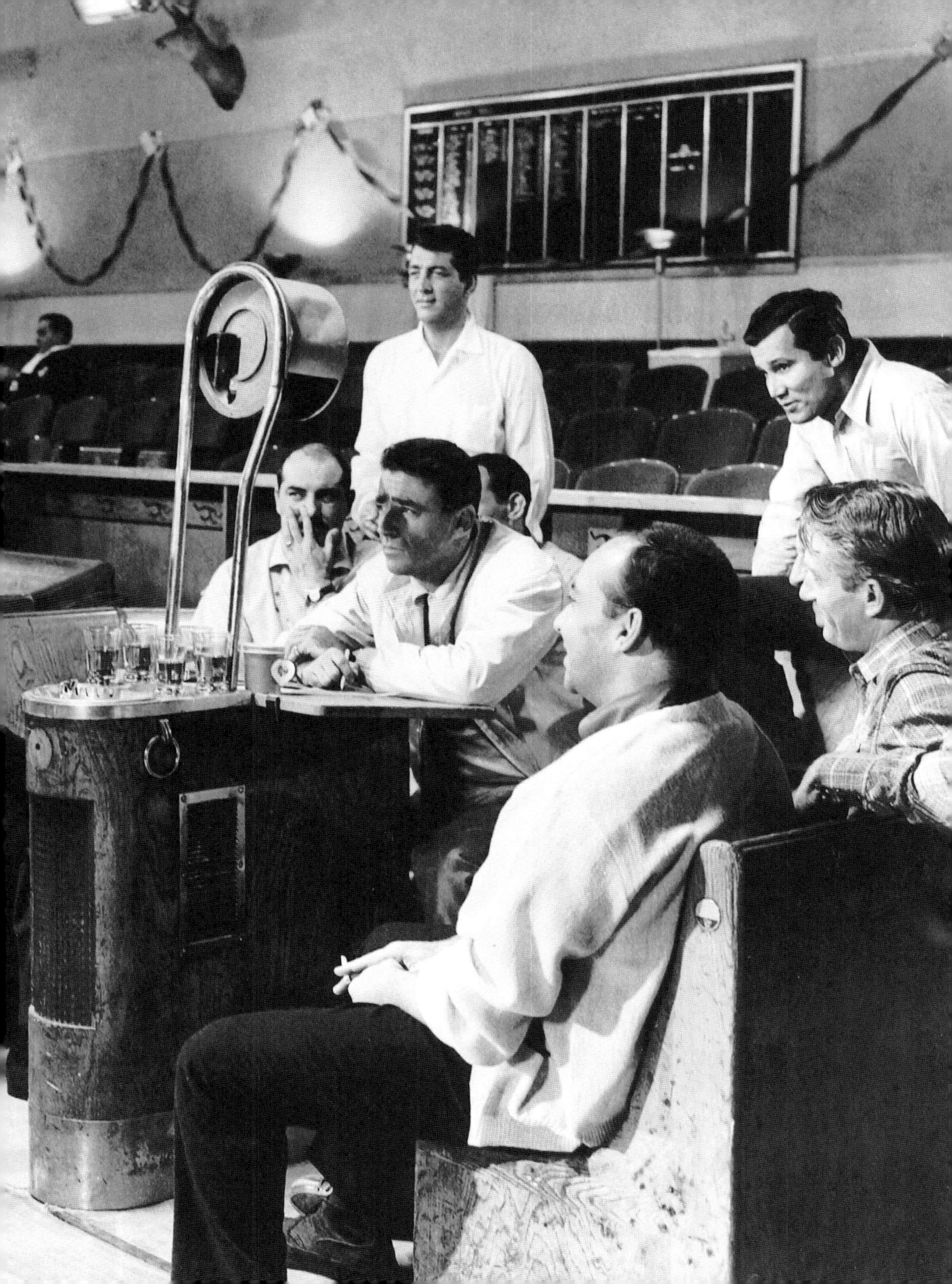

SINATRA, MARTIN, Lawford and Davis in *Ocean's Eleven.*

life: He was a thoroughly nocturnal man who lived in desperate fear of being alone. Drinking buddies and hangers-on (they were usually one and the same) were required, at the pain of Frank's displeasure, to stay up with him until the sky over Vegas lightened to the shade of morning twilight that he loved so much—"five o'clock Vegas blue," he called it. And woe be to the man who tried to sneak off to bed: Sinatra was known to roust the recalcitrant from their hotel rooms personally, sometimes with the aid of cherry bombs.

The single pass Frank issued to any of his drinking friends—and he issued it because there was no other choice—went to Dean Martin. "All the guys would take a steam bath, they'd go out and gamble—[and] Dean Martin would say, 'I'm sorry, guys, I'm going to bed,'" recalled famed Hollywood photographer Sid Avery, who was working on the set of *Ocean's Eleven.* "He'd get up early in the morning, go out and golf."

Sometimes Martin would soften the blow by telling Sinatra, "I've got a girl in my room"—and sometimes there really was a girl in his room. But then, and throughout his life, Dean Martin preferred his solitude. Despite his drunk act onstage (where the liquid in his glass was sometimes apple juice), he wasn't really a convivial drinker. He liked to watch a western on TV, get his beauty sleep and hit the links well rested. Golf was his one great passion in life.

So the image of the Rat Pack as a kind of floating social club, merrily cavorting together when the cameras weren't rolling, doesn't quite jibe with reality. Sometimes they gambled together, but the five of them didn't even all go to the legendary Sands steam bath (in which Frank had had the management install a craps table) together—incredibly, most times of the day, Sammy was barred from entering.

But Sinatra never lacked for nighttime companions. His usual entourage was always with him: Songwriter Jimmy Van Heusen; bodyguard/drinking buddies like Jilly Rizzo, Hank Sanicola and Al Silvani; and *Ocean's Eleven* cast members like Angie Dickinson, Richard Conte, Henry Silva, Buddy Lester, George Raft and Shirley MacLaine (who played a bit part as a Tipsy Girl) orbited around him, as did such visiting luminaries as Kirk Douglas, Yul Brynner and Steve Lawrence.

And then there was one very special new boon companion.

WARNER BROTHERS/ENTERTAINMENT PICTURES/ZUMA

THE GANG'S ALL HERE. From left: Richard Conte, Buddy Lester, Bishop, Davis, Sinatra, Martin, Lawford, Akim Tamiroff, Henry Silva, Richard Benedict, Norman Fell and Clem Harvey in *Ocean's Eleven*.

"Frank Sinatra introduced Sen. Kennedy at the Las Vegas Sands Hotel a couple of nights ago—and there was wild cheering from the audience. Then Dean Martin stepped from the wings and said to Sinatra, 'What was his name?' (Sammy Davis Jr.—appearing there with Sinatra, Martin, Peter Lawford and Joey Bishop also making the movie 'Ocean's 11'—collapsed from lack of oxygen and lack of sleep, and was ordered to rest.)"

—Earl Wilson's syndicated column of February 4, 1960

Frank Sinatra and John F. Kennedy may have first met as early as 1955, at a Democratic party rally; they almost certainly took note of each other at the 1956 Democratic Convention, where Sinatra sang the National Anthem and Kennedy lost out on a bid for the vice presidency—a loss that disassociated him from losing presidential candidate Adlai Stevenson and strategically positioned him for a presidential run in 1960. By 1958, when Frank reconciled with Peter Lawford, JFK's campaign was in full swing, and he made frequent trips to the key state of California, where he often encountered Sinatra at Peter and Pat Lawford's Santa Monica beach house.

The singer and the senator were drawn to each other immediately, each recognizing the other's magnetism and influence. For Sinatra, Kennedy had much of the same appeal as his idol Franklin Delano Roosevelt: He was an eastern patrician, witty and articulate, and coolly brilliant about the acquisition, maintenance and uses of power. Frank had been deeply impressed at the 1956 convention when he witnessed Kennedy and his organization instantly dismiss the senator's defeat and snap into gear for the next challenge. The idealistic Democrat in Sinatra believed John Kennedy would become President and that he possessed greatness. And Sinatra wanted to yoke his own great power to political power in Washington.

For his part, John F. Kennedy, as cultural historian Jonathan Gould writes, "was the first American President to be born in the twentieth century, the first to grow up in thrall to the movies, radio and the glossy idealizations of magazine advertising—the first American President to have his sensibility molded in the crucible of modern mass culture. In the young politician who emerged from this background, long-standing affinities between the political man and the theatrical man were combined to dazzling effect." As a now official presidential candidate—he formally announced on January 2, 1960—Kennedy recognized the power of show business, saw how it could help him in his campaign, and knew who the most powerful man in that business was. And as a man of powerful, if not insatiable, sexual appetites, Kennedy also recognized which show-business figure attracted more women than any other.

"Sinatra thought Kennedy was going to be a great President," says Ed Walters, who met the President-to-be on several occasions at the Sands. "Kennedy just wanted to get laid."

If the formulation is coarse, so was this side of John F. Kennedy. We are all divided souls; because he was rich and brilliant, with movie-star looks and charisma, and because he became a world-historical figure, Kennedy's contradictions stand out in especially stark contrast. He could be deeply thoughtful, sparklingly witty or serious; he could even be empathetic. But ultimately, where his personal life was concerned, he was a man who felt completely entitled to do precisely as he pleased, and pleasure was one of his highest values. All of which makes him an important part of the Rat Pack saga.

Jack Kennedy had learned well from his father, Joseph P. Kennedy, an enormously wealthy Boston

SINATRA WAS JUGGLING his singing career, the movie and the presidential campaign throughout 1960. On the opposite page, top, he shares a laugh with Pat Lawford, Pack associate Tony Curtis and Peter Lawford. The photograph was taken on July 1, and they are all enjoying the progress of JFK. Below: Election won, Sinatra is at the National Guard Armory building in Washington in January 1961, planning the Presidential Inaugural Ball festivities.

ED CLARK/LIFE/THE PICTURE COLLECTION

DENNIS STOCK/MAGNUM

banker and power broker who had made fortunes in investment banking and the liquor business, and, just before World War II, served as America's Ambassador to the Court of St. James's (he was forced to resign in disgrace after proclaiming that democracy was finished in England). The elder Kennedy had also been in the movie business: In the 1920s he had been a founder of the Hollywood studio RKO Pictures. Sex was one of the prerogatives of power for Joseph Kennedy, who took on managing the career of the star Gloria Swanson as an early movie project, and then took on Swanson herself as his mistress. There were many other women. Hollywood, with its ever-flowing stream of beautiful young actresses, and the hotel-casinos of Lake Tahoe and Las Vegas, with their plenteous showgirls and prostitutes, were the elder Kennedy's playgrounds, and his handsome second son soon set about following in his father's footsteps.

Jack Kennedy made his first visits to Hollywood before World War II as the glamorous and sought-after son of a famous father, and returned often as a rising politician and sun-loving sybarite, especially after acquiring a movie-star brother-in-law in the mid-1950s. Peter Lawford's reconciliation with Frank Sinatra only sweetened the deal. By mid-1959, the singer, having been vigorously lobbied by Joe Kennedy, was deeply involved in JFK's presidential campaign. In November 1959, after attending a Democratic fund-raiser in Los Angeles, the candidate stayed at Frank's house in Palm Springs—an event Sinatra memorialized by having a plaque placed on the door of the bedroom in which the future President slept. It is highly unlikely that Kennedy slept alone. Sinatra's pleasure palace on Wonder Palms Road was the bachelor pad of bachelor pads, home to an unending round of parties and a constant parade of female visitors, from lady friends to paid companions. Songwriter Van Heusen often helped the singer find both amateur and professional company, as did Lawford. "I was Frank's pimp, and Frank was Jack's," the actor confessed, many years later. "It sounds terrible now, but then it was a lot of fun."

The fun continued. Flying west on his campaign plane the *Caroline* in early February of 1960, Kennedy and his entourage (including his 27-year-old brother, Ted) stopped in Las Vegas and stayed for several nights at the Sands, as Sinatra's guest. "There was no goddamn reason for stopping there except fun and games," a CBS reporter traveling with the candidate recalled. On the other hand, "We all figured, 'How bad can it be to catch Sinatra at the Sands?'"

That was the whole thing in a nutshell. In an era when the (almost exclusively male) press corps covering politicians and candidates winked at sexual peccadilloes, Jack Kennedy had carte blanche. He attended several of the Summit shows, where Sinatra would introduce him fulsomely from the audience: "Ladies and gentlemen, Senator John F. Kennedy, from the great state of Massachusetts . . . The next President of the United States!" A blurry home movie taken on one of those nights shows the slim young senator grinning and standing to take a bow. Then Dean Martin would lurch out, holding a glass of apple juice and slurring his words: "Whadja say his name was?" The audience, including Kennedy, howled every time.

After one of the shows, there was a private party in Sinatra's suite; the candidate and some of his entourage were present, as were at least two young women. Two reporters who were there excused themselves, one of them later recalled, "because we sensed that Jack and Frank and a couple of the girls were about to have a party." One of the women, Judith Campbell, a striking and wholesome-looking 26-year-old with dark hair and blue eyes, had been involved with Sinatra for a couple of months. (Though a number of people, including Sinatra's valet George Jacobs, have alleged that Campbell accepted money for her companionship, she always vociferously maintained—and kept the receipts to prove—that she paid her own way.) And before Senator Kennedy flew on to Oregon, he, too, had begun *(continued on page 77)*

A TRIO BOUND FOR DISUNION, because of the unseen but never unfelt presence of the Mafia, was Sinatra, Kennedy and Lawford, seen opposite, top, during the inaugural gala in January 1961. Bottom, enjoying the entertainment on the night before the inauguration, are Sinatra and Lawford. Later in Vegas, in a famous incident after Lawford had been emphatically cut out of the entire Rat Pack equation because the President had emphatically cut ties with Sinatra, Frank refused to take the stage during a performance until Peter had been removed from the audience.

© PHIL STERN, PHILIP STERN TRUST

LEONARD MCCOMBE/LIFE/THE PICTURE COLLECTION

PAUL SCHUTZER/LIFE/THE PICTURE COLLECTION

BETTMANN/GETTY

THE IN-LAWS Jackie Kennedy and Peter Lawford are all smiles at the Inaugural Ball, above. Opposite: Sinatra escorts Mrs. Kennedy to the inaugural gala—organized, produced and staged by him, and featuring the talents of many of his friends as well as the orchestrations of his indispensable collaborator and bandleader Nelson Riddle. Sinatra and Co. had already given much to the cause, and the gala, too, would raise funds to pay for the now-ended campaign.

STAIR-4

a relationship with Campbell, one that would continue into his presidency—and would be further complicated by the fact that Judith Campbell would soon also be sleeping with Sam Giancana, to whom Sinatra introduced her that March, when the Summit briefly took its act to Miami's Fontainebleau Hotel.

On January 28, 1960, in the midst of the shooting of *Ocean's Eleven,* and a couple of days before John Kennedy arrived in Vegas, Frank Sinatra flew to Los Angeles to record a campaign song for the candidate. The tune, a special-lyrics version of "High Hopes," a number that Sammy Cahn and Jimmy Van Heusen had written for a recent Sinatra movie, was called "High Hopes with Jack Kennedy." It began:

Everyone is voting for Jack.
'Cause he's got what all the rest lack.
Everyone wants to back Jack,
Jack is on the right track.

'Cause he's got High Hopes!
He's got High Hopes!
1960's the year for his High Hopes!

From January to November, Sinatra campaigned for Kennedy like a man possessed, singing at fund-raisers, leaning on the wealthy for contributions, rallying his fellow celebrities to the cause. Peter Lawford and Sammy Davis Jr., who was also a fervent JFK supporter, frequently appeared with him. Dean Martin, who was cynical about politicians in general, and about Kennedy in particular, was conspicuously absent.

Sinatra might have done well to cultivate a little more cynicism. That April, a curious item appeared in Dorothy Kilgallen's syndicated gossip column:

It's mighty puzzling to members of Hollywood's famous Rat Pack, but intimates of Senator Jack Kennedy say the handsome presidential candidate keeps disavowing any close friendship with Frank Sinatra and insists any publicity linking the singer with his campaign must have been "planted" by the Sinatra interests. They quote him as saying he's only met the singer "a few times" and protesting that Frank is brother-in-law Peter Lawford's pal, not his.

The item was doubly striking: For one thing, it may have marked the first use in print of the term "Rat Pack" as applied to the members of the Summit. For another, there was that strange and chilling, albeit anonymous, assertion of Kennedy's disaffection toward Sinatra. And while it must be noted that there was no love lost between Frank and Kilgallen—she seemed to particularly enjoy needling him in print (and probably knew well how he would hate the Rat Pack label); he used to refer to her, onstage, as "that chinless wonder"—it's doubtful that the columnist made her item up out of whole cloth. A number of people close to John Kennedy were extremely uneasy about his palling around with a man who palled around with hookers and gangsters. One of the uneasiest was the candidate's brother Robert Kennedy.

And yet Sinatra, Lawford and Davis continued their joint campaigning unabated. Frank, in all likelihood needling Kilgallen back, came up with a new label for the three of them: the Jack Pack.

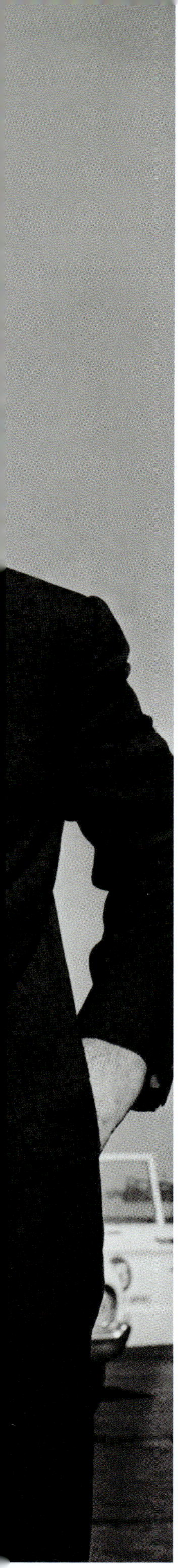

BEFORE THE QUIET firestorm in Palm Springs that led to Peter's exile and Frank's rest-of-life enmity for the Kennedy clan, Sinatra, Lawford and U.S. Attorney General Robert F. Kennedy seem happy enough as they wait for a helicopter to take them to a July 1961 fund-raising dinner for a hospital in Los Angeles. The advantage of history allows us to know that Jack Kennedy wasn't Frank's enemy: Bobby was. FBI chief J. Edgar Hoover came to hate RFK, mob boss Sam Giancana (in concert with all mob bosses) came to hate RFK, and certainly Frank Sinatra was in Bobby's crosshairs as soon as JFK was inaugurated and appointed RFK as A.G. Lawford was hardly oblivious, but he was characteristically powerless to affect events.

BETTMANN/GETTY

The world premiere of *Ocean's Eleven* took place—where else?—in Las Vegas, at midnight on August 3, 1960. The cocktail party, dinner party and Summit reunion leading up to the opening made for a Vegas blowout to top all Vegas blowouts, attended by the dozens of stars who'd descended on the gambling mecca for the premiere, which was televised on Jack Paar's *Tonight* show. Frank, Peter and Sammy joined Dean (who was already appearing at the Copa Room) and Joey (who'd flown in from a Chicago gig) for the show, which pulled out all the stops. "[T]heir horsing around with race and religion has finally gotten out of hand," complained Las Vegas *Sun* columnist Ralph Pearl. "Mix an abundance of blue material with that and you have an inflammable situation."

The movie itself was sedate by comparison. To watch it today is a strange experience—especially in light of the George Clooney–Brad Pitt–Matt Damon remakes, two out of three of which are far more fun than the original. The 1960 film's story moves along breezily and stylishly as its multiple-casino-robbing plot proceeds, but the picture can't quite make up its mind whether it's a comedy or a drama: What else can you say about a caper starring Frank Sinatra in which Sinatra neither smiles nor sings? (The only Rat Packer who truly seems to be enjoying himself is Sammy Davis Jr. as that singing, dancing garbage man.) The movie's chief charms are visual: The opening credits by the great graphic designer Saul Bass are terrific, and cinematographer William H. Daniels's vivid, dynamic rendering of the casinos and their denizens make you realize just how compelling, how *fun*, a place the small-town, gangster-run, pre-corporate Vegas could be.

What's far less compelling—to a present-day viewer, at any rate—is *Ocean's Eleven*'s vision of manhood, 1960-style. Why were the wartime buddies robbing the casinos? Not just for the money, but, as Tom Santopietro notes, to "inject some sorely needed excitement into their postwar lives, which had been disappointing in their blandness and rigidity." The same might be said, Santopietro writes, for the audiences who flocked to see the Rat Pack in Vegas, and the movie they made: "Onstage and onscreen, Frank Sinatra and friends were living out the fantasies of all middle-aged men who felt trapped in marriage, suburbia and playing by the rules. They were men who wanted their freedom back."

Fair enough—in fantasy anyway—but what about the women who were the other side of the equation? The females in the film are mostly just ornaments or adjuncts, easily ordered around and put in their place, as when Sinatra's character, Danny Ocean, tells his estranged wife, played by Angie Dickinson, "Now just sit there and don't interrupt me." Or as when Danny walks into a room where Lawford's character is being massaged by a blonde in short shorts and tells her and her similarly blonde friend, "Okay, girls—time for your nap. Beat it." Or, most startlingly, when Dean Martin's character announces he's going to go into politics. His platform? "Repeal the Fourteenth [sic] and the Twentieth Amendment—take the vote away from the women, make slaves out of 'em."

In real life, none of the Rat Packers enjoyed such commanding or tidy relations with the opposite sex. Both Joey and Dean had been married since the 1940s and had spent much of their lives on the road; infer what you will. Peter Lawford, who had been fitfully employed and frequently unfaithful since his 1954 marriage to Pat Kennedy, had fallen in his wife's estimation as her family's political fortunes rose. And while Frank Sinatra, in the midst of his most prolonged period of bachelorhood, was flying high—artistically, financially, sexually—he still carried a torch for Ava Gardner, the love of his life, and battled constantly against the demons that always threatened. He was the creator and leader of the Clan, or the Summit, or the Rat Pack—but he was also the one who needed the group most of all. The fun of his epic bachelorhood was long and loud and real, but there was also a desperate, million-miles-an-hour quality to it—a lunar loneliness just beneath the surface.

Only Sammy, about to be married to the Swedish actress May Britt, had stars in his eyes.

In an era when segregation still held the South in a vise grip and black-white relations in the rest of America hadn't progressed much further, interracial romance, not to mention marriage, was widely viewed as an abomination. In the mid-1950s Davis had been widely censured—by blacks as well as

EVERETT

UNITED ARTISTS/REX/SHUTTERSTOCK

BEYOND THE STURM und drang of politics and grudges and enmities of real-world personal interactions, there were careers to be pursued, there was money to be made. *Ocean's Eleven* had made plenty, and so: *Sergeants 3*, a 1962 remake of *Gunga Din* that would be the only other film to feature all five of the Rat Packers. Above: In the movie, Dino Martini pours. At left, more amusing by half, milk seems to be the drink of choice.

SINATRA WAS PRODUCER of ***Sergeants 3*** **and had a stake in all of what are historically considered Pack films, each of which featured a number in the title:** ***Ocean's Eleven, 4 for Texas*** **(1963, no Sammy, Peter or Joey) and** ***Robin and the 7 Hoods*** **(1964, no Peter or Joey). He was very clear-eyed about numbers. "Of course, they're not great movies, no one could claim that," he later said. "But every movie I've made through my own company has made money."**

whites—for his affair with blonde bombshell Kim Novak. Ultimately, Harry Cohn, the head of Columbia Pictures, had a mob friend briefly abduct Sammy to frighten him into breaking off the relationship. By the time Davis fell in love with the equally blonde Britt, in 1959, he had become a lightning rod for intolerance: Taking the stage to sing the National Anthem at the 1960 Democratic Convention in Los Angeles, he was booed by members of the Mississippi and Alabama delegations. He finished the anthem in tears.

In deference to the Kennedy campaign, Sammy postponed his highly controversial wedding to May Britt until after the election. In return for his loyalty, Davis was disinvited from the Kennedy inauguration gala. Frank Sinatra had orchestrated the starry celebration, which featured patriotic music conducted by Leonard Bernstein and a poem recited by Robert Frost, as well as appearances by Laurence Olivier, Gene Kelly, Shirley MacLaine, Ethel Merman, Jimmy Durante, Milton Berle and Bette Davis. The gala also featured such black luminaries as Harry Belafonte, Sidney Poitier, Nat King Cole and Mahalia Jackson—but none of them was in the newspapers at the time for the unforgivable sin of marrying outside their race.

When the President-elect's secretary Evelyn Lincoln phoned Sammy to ask him to bow out of the gala because of the political damage it might do to Kennedy, he was crushed. He would remain permanently disaffected from the Democratic Party, eventually turning his loyalties to the very man John F. Kennedy had very narrowly defeated in the 1960 election, Richard Nixon.

Sammy wasn't the only one who felt used by the Kennedys. During the campaign, the Machiavellian Joseph P. Kennedy had prevailed upon Frank Sinatra to ask his pal Sam Giancana to help with the perilously tight West Virginia primary by spreading strategic cash among Democratic ward bosses and voters: the ploy won the primary for JFK. During the election, Frank called upon Giancana for similar help with the mobster's closely contested home turf of Cook County, Illinois. It is not clear if specific quid pro quo was promised, but Giancana's assumption all along was that after Kennedy won, the FBI would lay off the Chicago mob. The opposite occurred. Soon after the inauguration, President Kennedy appointed his brother Robert, a sworn enemy of organized crime, as his attorney general. The federal government would hound Sam Giancana for the rest of his life. Sinatra, his daughter Tina wrote, had "gone to Giancana out of friendship for Jack Kennedy and expected nothing back. What he did *not* expect was to be set up like a blindsided innocent, like a fool to take the fall."

BETTMANN/GETTY

Sam Giancana was furious. And he would make Frank pay. Dean and Sammy would have to chip in, too.

"*Ocean's Eleven* . . . was among the more famous of the Rat Pack films, but there were also nearly a dozen others," a popular-history website solemnly informs us. In fact, there were exactly three others. In reality, *Ocean's Eleven* was the original and most famous Rat Pack movie, and just one other picture featured the entire five-man crew: 1962's *Sergeants 3* was a Western based on Rudyard Kipling's poem "Gunga Din." Like *Ocean's Eleven,* it was visually beautiful, fitfully comic and, in general, an excuse for the quintet to fool around onscreen and reprise their respective shticks, this time in U.S. Cavalry uniforms: Frank was the wisecracking leader, Dean the easygoing sidekick; Sammy was the happy, singing and dancing one; Joey was the glum, monosyllabic one; and once again, Peter was the spoiled rich boy.

The act, fresh and naughty for a few months in 1960, was already getting stale around the edges. The critics noticed it: "[Sinatra's] Cub Scout troupe are pioneering in a new art form: the 4-million-dollar home movie," sniped *Variety.* But for the time being, the public was still buying it—*Sergeants 3* performed quite respectably at the box office. And Vegas still loved it. A Sands marquee of the era read:

Dean Martin
Maybe Frank – Maybe Sammy

And Peter and Joey? Well, they had never been headliners after all, and within a year or two, both were history as far as Frank was concerned. Peter was first to go. In March of 1962, Brother-in-Lawford committed the final, unpardonable sin—although ultimately he was really just the whipping boy for John F. Kennedy. That month, the President scheduled a trip to California, and his plan was to spend a relaxing few days at Frank Sinatra's Palm Springs house. Frank, anticipating that his place in the sun would become a kind of Western White House, had had extensive renovations done, including installing extra phone lines and a helipad. But when the attorney general found out where his brother meant to stay, he quickly interceded. Bobby Kennedy knew that Sam Giancana had been a guest at the Palm Springs house a number of times; and in all likelihood he knew about Judith Campbell, the mutual girlfriend of the mob boss and the Chief Executive. Speaking of Sinatra, Robert Kennedy told his brother: "Johnny, you just can't associate with this guy."

And Lawford was chosen to deliver the bad news to the hot-tempered Chairman of the Board. In fact, the news was worse than bad: On the pretext that the Secret Service had declared Sinatra's place difficult to secure, the President would stay instead at the Palm Springs house of Bing Crosby, Frank's rival as Greatest American Singer, and an arch-Republican.

Frank had the predictable explosion. And that was it for Peter.

Spain

FORMOSA: Let's show 'em. Let's show those asshole Hollywood fruitcakes that they can't get away with it as if nothing's happened. Let's hit Sinatra. Or I could whack out a couple of those other guys. Lawford and that Martin, and I could take the n----- [Davis] and put his other eye out.

GIANCANA: No . . . I've got other plans for them.

—from a 1962 FBI wiretap of the gangsters Johnny Formosa and Sam Giancana

That November, just a few weeks after the world had come close to destruction in the Cuban Missile Crisis, the core of the Rat Pack, Frank and Dean and Sammy, played a series of command performances at a nightclub just outside Chicago called the Villa Venice. The recently renovated Villa Venice was a splendid establishment on several acres in Wheeling, Illinois: Gondolas steered by costumed gondoliers (and on the evenings in question, crewed by prostitutes) plied man-made canals; the Italianate showroom, a symphony in red leather, marble and gilt, was magnificent; and in a Quonset hut just off-site, there was a complete (and thoroughly illegal—and rigged) casino.

And command performances were precisely what the trio gave: The owner-operator of the Villa Venice was Sam Giancana; and Frank, Dean and Sammy, each of them used to making five figures a week in Vegas, were working gratis. (Sinatra alone stood to make any money from the deal—his new record label, Reprise, was taping the shows for a live LP. The album was never released.) It was payback time: for the West Virginia primary, for the votes in Cook County, for the broken promises of the Kennedys. Not to mention for all the help the mobster had given all three entertainers over the not always smooth course of their respective careers.

And as always—especially for Sammy, who had periodically been bossed, bullied and even physically assaulted by Giancana—there was the implicit threat of what could happen to an entertainer, even a major star, if he didn't toe the line. When FBI agents, interviewing Davis in his Chicago hotel room, asked him why he had turned aside lucrative nightclub gigs to work for free, he offered to fix them a drink, then took one himself.

"Baby, that's a very good question," Davis said. "But I have to say it's for my man Francis."

"Or friends of his?"

"By all means."

"Like Sam Giancana?"

"By all means."

The agents asked Davis to elaborate. "Baby, let me say this," the entertainer said. "I got one eye, and that one eye sees a lot of things that my brain tells me I shouldn't talk about. Because my brain says that if I do, my one eye might not be seeing anything after a while."

On opening night at Villa Venice, Dean Martin walked out onto the showroom floor, glass in hand, and after delivering his usual line ("How long I been on?"), began to sing a parody of "When You're Smiling"—

When you're drinking, when you're drinkin',
The show looks good to you . . .

He then segued into a takeoff (special lyrics by Sammy Cahn) on "The Lady Is a Tramp":

I love Chicago, it's carefree and gay,
I'd even work here without any pay,
I'll lay you odds it turns out that way,
That's why this gentleman is a tramp . . .

The laughter from the audience—which besides Giancana included the mobsters Joe Fischetti, Jim DeGeorge, Marshall Caifano, Jimmy "The Monk" Allegretti, Felix "Milwaukee Phil" Alderisio and Willie "Potatoes" Daddano—was masculine and chilling. *(continued on page 88)*

SAM GIANCANA RIVALED his "friend" Sinatra for number of nicknames: Sammy, Sam the Cigar, Mooney, most often, Momo. In this May 19, 1965, photograph, he is seen walking into a courthouse in Chicago to testify before a federal grand jury looking into underworld activities. He was hot at this time and high profile, and would shortly go into exile outside the country. A decade later, upon returning, he would still be hot and too high profile, and would be offed by suspects unknown.

AP

BETTMANN/GETTY

SINATRA HAD PALS in the Mafia; this is, by now, well established. One photograph, seen at left, launched a thousand questions at the time, many of them from federal investigators: Why would Sinatra, after decades of denying mob links, pose backstage at the Westchester Premier Theatre in New York with (standing, third from right) Carlo Gambino and his friends? Politeness, was Sinatra's answer under oath. "Mr. Gambino had arrived with his granddaughter, whose name happened to be Sinatra . . . and they'd like to take a picture. I said, 'Fine.' They came in and they took a picture of the little girl, and before I realized what happened, there were approximately eight or nine men around me . . . I didn't even know their names, let alone their backgrounds." Okay, but he certainly knew the background of Judith Campbell, below, girlfriend of both Sam Giancana and John F. Kennedy—which was a problem, a big problem.

AP

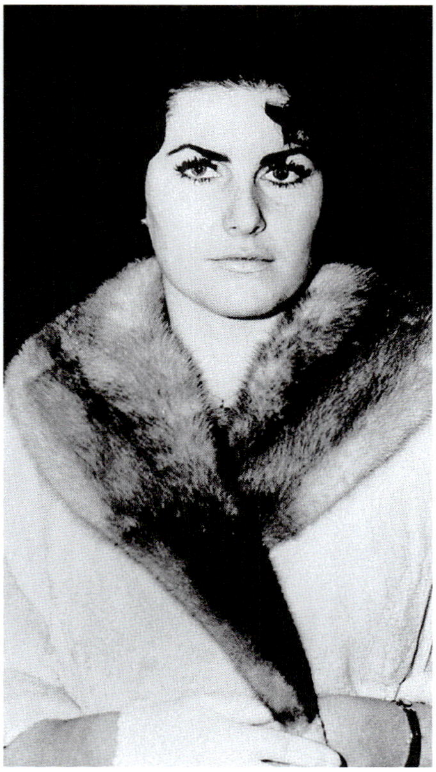

EVERETT

IT IS SIMPLY IRRESISTIBLE to follow the photos of Sinatra's real-world mob friends with this group shot from the 1964 gangster film *Robin and the 7 Hoods,* which featured Dean, Frank, Hank Henry and Sammy. Bing Crosby and Peter Falk were also in the flick, which concerned the rackets in Chicago—Momo Giancana's town!—in the Prohibition era. It's funny, truly funny, the degree to which the Rat Pack ethos overlapped that of mobdom: the multiple nicknames, the tough/cool attitudes, Frank's sense of *omertà,* the alternative wordings for everything in the world—a whole other language. Rarely if ever in either sphere would a man simply be called a man, a woman a woman or a five-dollar bill a five-dollar bill. If you wanted to speak to a Rat Packer, a foreknowledge of the lexicon was useful. A quick alphabetical primer: A *broad* was a sexy woman. *Charlies* were sexy breasts. A *chick* was a young sexy woman. A *clyde* was any kind of thing. *Crazy* meant cool. A *crumb* was a creep. *Gasoline* was, as we've noted, booze. A *gasser* was a great person. A *harve* was a square. A *mouse* was a small woman. A *player* was a gambler imbued with brio. *Ring-a-ding* meant terrific. A *twirl* was a chick who loved to dance. And the suffix *-ville* had many uses: bombsville, endsville, splitsville.

The Rat Pack movies—*Ocean's Eleven, Sergeants 3, 4 for Texas* and *Robin and the 7 Hoods*—are all identifiable by a craps-significant number in the title. But in the case of the two Westerns of the bunch, three plus four equals snake eyes. Like *Sergeants 3,* 1963's *4 for Texas* (which despite the title included only two Rat Packers, Sinatra and Martin) was a mess—if possible, an even bigger mess than the earlier picture. It had a little bit of everything—western action, spoof and love story—adding up to not much. *Time*'s reviewer opined that the movie was

> *. . . one of those pictures that are known in Hollywood as Clanbakes . . . Unfortunately they are not much fun to see . . . What's mainly wrong with "Texas," though, is what's wrong with all Clan pictures: the attitude of the people on the screen. They constitute an in-group and they seem bored with the outside world. Sometimes, perish the thought, they even are obviously bored with each other . . . They appear less concerned to entertain the public than to indulge their private fantasies.*

Frank Sinatra, having grown up short and slight and Italian-American in an era when that ethnicity was near the bottom of the social scale, had long nourished his own not-so-private fantasy. "Frank wanted to be a hood," his friend the singer Eddie Fisher recalled. "He once said, 'I'd rather be a don of the Mafia than President of the United States.' I don't think he was fooling."

In *Robin and the 7 Hoods* (1964), an amiable musical comedy set in 1920s Chicago and the best of the Rat Pack movies—arguably not a great distinction—Sinatra finally got to live out his fantasy, playing a mobster, albeit a comic one (Robbo by name), for the first and only time in his film career. But as *Robin* went into *(continued on page 94)*

THEY WERE ONLY a little older, but you could tell they were getting older. On the set of *4 for Texas* in 1963 are Frank and Dino, going over lines with dialogue coach Bob Sherman (left). The film featured not only Anita Ekberg, Ursula Andress and Charles Bronson but also the Three Stooges. Six degrees of separation with the Rat Pack would extend to the ends of the earth.

EVERETT

THE

BETTMANN/GETTY

THERE WAS NO TELLING in the early 1950s what Vegas might be in a decade, but wow—look what became of it. Celebrating the 11th anniversary of the Sands on December 15, 1963, are the big three of the Pack plus, at top, entertainers Danny Thomas and Lucille Ball, at far right Gary Morton, Lucy's husband, and at far left Jack Entratter. Entratter was the president of the Sands, but he was no mere club manager. Having started as a doorman at the Stork Club in New York City, he had worked his way up and eventually became a co-owner of the Copacabana. In 1952, he was tapped by a Texas oilman who was the principal behind the Sands to be entertainment director of the new casino and hotel in Vegas. The ebullient six-foot-four Entratter headed west, and started phoning his many friends among the nation's biggest entertainers: those seen here and also Lena Horne, Jerry Lewis, Red Skelton, Alan King, Steve Lawrence and Eydie Gorme. The Copa Room became the place to be, and Entratter was the man to know. His name came before the word "presents" on posters, and even for Sinatra gigs the credit ran "created and staged by Jack Entratter." Specifically regarding the Rat Pack, it was Entratter who came up with the idea of Joey Bishop presiding as a kind of staid master of ceremonies. Sinatra routinely name-checked him from the stage, often in vulgar Rat Pack fashion, even incorporating his name into ad-libbed lyrics. Entratter as much as anyone made Vegas what it became until, after a 15-year reign in 1967, the Sands was sold to Howard Hughes, who of course had his own ideas.

ESTATE OF JOHN BRYSON/SYGMA/GETTY

MARTIN AND SINATRA, **their relationship always complicated, would never split. If Dean needed a shuttle on the Lear between Vegas and L.A., Frank would accommodate. How do we know that's Sinatra's plane? Well, the stripe tells us much. Sinatra's pajamas, donned at dawn, were orange. His house in Palm Springs was decorated in orange. His favorite sweaters were orange. Sinatra's was a bright, bold, orange life. "Pocket handkerchiefs are optional," he once said, handing out sartorial advice. "But I always wear one. Usually orange, since orange is my favorite color." The Rat Pack never had an official banner or flag, but if it had, there is little question what the principal color would have been. Just by the way: Dean's favorite color was blue. But then, his favorite singer was Bing Crosby. As said, the relationship was complicated. Nevertheless, it endured. Because it did—because there was no official estrangement as with Sinatra and Lawford—there were occasional calls for a "Rat Pack Reunion," or at least a gathering of the core members.**

LEAR JET

production in the fall of 1963, real life was colliding with Frank's Mafia daydreams.

Sam Giancana, who wore Sinatra's friendship ring, had long socialized with the singer: The two men traveled together, boozed and whored together, played practical jokes together (throwing cherry bombs at people was their favorite). But the one place the two men were officially forbidden to socialize in was Frank's Vegas home base, the hotel-casino in which he owned a 9 percent share, the Sands. This was because as one of 11 men on the Nevada Gaming Control Board's Excluded Person List—the so-called Black Book—Giancana was legally enjoined from setting foot in any casino in the state.

The mobster had long skirted the rule by vacationing, as Frank Sinatra's guest, at a Lake Tahoe establishment in which Sinatra also owned points, a hotel-casino called the Cal-Neva Lodge. As its name indicates, the Cal-Neva straddles the state line, which was designed right into a carpet in the main lodge. The hotel facilities are on one side of the border, the casino on the other (gambling was legal in only one state in the union, Nevada). Technically speaking, Sam Giancana shouldn't have ever been near the Cal-Neva at all, but since he was adept at lying low, no one took any notice.

This all changed in July of 1963, when Giancana got involved in a fistfight at the resort; the police were called, and the incident became a matter of public record. The fact that the mobster had been Sinatra's guest did not go down well with the Nevada Gaming Control Board, which in September officially charged the singer with violating the statute that forbade any licensee from "catering to persons of notorious, unsavory reputation." The Board summoned Sinatra to a hearing, but that October, rather than face the very public pillorying such an inquest would have brought him, Frank surrendered his gaming license and sold his share in Cal-Neva, as well as his precious nine points in the Sands. The clubhouse now belonged to others, and where was the fun in that?

Strikingly, Frank Sinatra's daughter Nancy has asserted that her father gave up his casino shares without a fight not only to avoid the negative fallout of being publicly associated with Giancana but also because he "would not allow his self-interests to hurt John Kennedy." John Kennedy had hurt Frank Sinatra grievously, cutting him off (much as he also cut off Judith Campbell) without a second thought, to steer clear of any whiff of mob influence. But Sinatra, who would always revere the 35th President,

LEONARD MCCOMBE/LIFE/THE PICTURE COLLECTION

IT WAS ENDING even before John Kennedy was assassinated in November 1963. Lawford was out. Bishop was gone. Sinatra and the Kennedys weren't speaking. Giancana was angry with the Kennedys and was getting into duke-outs in Nevada, causing problems for his friends. And then Kennedy was killed. Right: Sammy, a good man who had been treated harshly by the President when he had been banished from the inauguration ceremonies because of his prominent marriage to the white May Britt, visits the grave site in Arlington National Cemetery.

LEONARD MCCOMBE/LIFE/THE PICTURE COLLECTION

chose instead to blame Bobby Kennedy and Peter Lawford.

The Rat Pack's diminution continued. Producer Sinatra of course excluded Lawford from *Robin and the 7 Hoods;* oddly enough, he also cut out Joey Bishop, with whom he was in the midst of some kind of mini-feud. An odd addition—but then Sinatra always operated by his own set of rules—was Bing Crosby, the very man whose Palm Springs residence Kennedy had chosen over Frank's, costarring as Allen A. Dale, Robbo's minister of finance. Of course, Crosby was a big star and a great singer, and his casting served Sinatra's interests. The combination of the four terrific voices of Frank, Bing, Sammy and Dean singing some wonderful songs by Sammy Cahn and Jimmy Van Heusen (including the classic "My Kind of Town") makes *Robin*, mostly, a surprisingly pleasant movie to watch.

The movie was still in production on November 21, 1963, when, as cast and crew were shooting on location in a Los Angeles cemetery, Sinatra leaned against a tombstone for a cigarette break and started as he noticed the inscription: JOHN F. KENNEDY, 1873–1940. The next day, as filming proceeded on the Warner Bros. lot, the news came in from Dallas. The memory of the gravestone would haunt Sinatra ever afterward.

It may be pat to say that the Rat Pack ended on November 22, 1963, but it wouldn't be off the mark to note that the particular epoch of American masculinity embodied by Frank, Dean, Sammy, Peter, Joey and Jack Kennedy, not to mention James Bond and Don Draper—the era of skinny ties and narrow-lapelled suits and endless rounds of cigarettes and whiskey and guiltless sex—was rapidly drawing to some kind of close as that *(continued on page 100)*

GOING SOLO, all of the Pack members did fine—except, perhaps, Peter Lawford, who devolved into more of a "celebrity" than a movie star, generating his biggest headlines by marrying women much younger than himself. Sammy, for his part, extended his stardom on Broadway, and here is seen in his dressing room in 1964 during his run in the hit production of *Golden Boy*.

JOHN DOMINIS/LIFE/THE PICTURE COLLECTION

THE LEADER OF THE PACK was always Sinatra, and in the aftermath he continued to be the biggest star. He would make many more movies, some of them pretty good if nothing as fine as *The Man with the Golden Arm* or *The Manchurian Candidate*. He would of course continue to sing, generating hit albums and singles for his own record label and even climbing to the top of the charts with a duet featuring his beloved daughter Nancy. He would remain the undisputed king of Las Vegas whenever he encamped there. He would marry a couple more times—Mia Farrow, of all people, and then finally and forever, Barbara Marx—and would even return to the White House, this time at the invitation of a Republican, his fellow Hollywood veteran Ronald Reagan. He would, as we will see on the next several pages, bump into his old Packmates along the way. How could he not? It had always been about the orbit. They were in one another's orbit, as he had once made certain he was in Bogie's. They continued to be in one another's orbit. The rings grew wider and they drifted apart, then suddenly they circled back and were there again—in passing.

dark year ended and a strange new year began, a year that was little more than a month old when a still despairing country shook its head in disbelief at the sight of the four young Englishmen making improbably joyous music on Ed Sullivan's stage.

Nineteen sixty-four was the year everything changed, when rock 'n' roll—which, few remember, had almost been counted out after a chastened Elvis returned from the Army in 1960—simply took over, and Frank and Dean and Sammy, their act together so fresh and shocking just a few years before, were well on their way to being old news. When *Robin and the 7 Hoods* was released in June, it already had the look of a cultural relic: *A Hard Day's Night* would come out just six weeks later. And while none of the Rat Pack issued a formal declaration of dissolution, a gossip column in July would note, almost as an afterthought: "The group is broken up now . . ."

Leaving so little behind: a legacy of naughty fun in Las Vegas that, in reality, would last just three more years, until Howard Hughes and the corporations displaced the mob and took over the casinos. Three mostly joyless movies and one fairly good one—only two of the films featuring the full poker hand of five men. Some blurry black-and-white footage of the act, with a lot of puzzling hilarity about alcohol and many cringeworthy wisecracks about the color of Sammy Davis Jr.'s skin.

And yet the phrase shimmers in the air like a heat mirage over the Las Vegas desert—the desert of the old days, when the tumbleweeds blew between the casinos spread out along Route 91, and the coyotes and the high-rollers howled at the moon—*Rat Pack*. Two words to conjure with, and a reminder that legend always trumps fact, especially when truth has been scattered with the sands of time.

You had to be there.

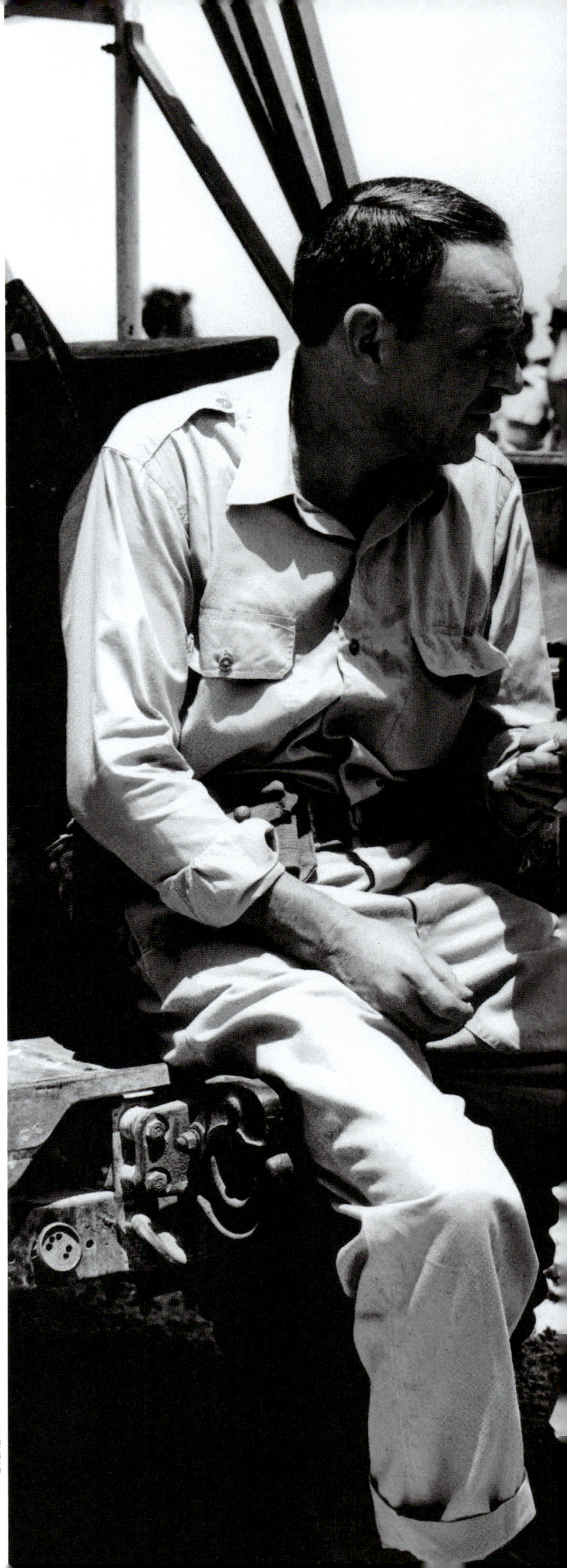

IN 1966, Sinatra and Kirk Douglas found themselves back together during the making of the big-budget *Cast a Giant Shadow*. They had both been great friends of Humphrey Bogart, and Douglas had been on the periphery of both Rat Packs. He would outlast them all, proving perhaps that it was better—or at least safer—to be slightly outside than well inside.

EVERETT

AT A 1965 BENEFIT performance in St. Louis hosted by Johnny Carson (right), Martin, Davis and Sinatra have clearly channeled the old Pack spirit.

CBS/GETTY

WARNER BROTHERS/EVERETT

HAPPY TOGETHER was always the later-in-life theme for Dean, Sammy, Shirley and Frank, even when the circumstance that might cause the reunion was something like the filming in 1984 of *Cannonball Run II*, a film that would make *Ocean's Eleven* look like *Citizen Kane*. Martin, Davis and MacLaine had what might politely be called real roles in the movie, and Sinatra one of a thousand cameos, but no matter: On the set, it was old home week. This would be the last time either Martin or Sinatra would appear in a feature film; Davis would soldier on briefly, and of course MacLaine's venerability, even unto *Downton Abbey*, is legendary. It's interesting: Sinatra, yielding to changing times and tastes, first announced his retirement from show business in 1971—setting the stage for a record-breaking string of comebacks. Among them was a final Rat Pack tour, a planned 29-city affair in 1988. (On the pages immediately following, the trio rehearses in March of that year at Davis's house in Beverly Hills.) Sinatra would sing almost until his death in 1998 at age 82, recording a couple of best-selling duets discs in his final years. Martin would live until 1995 when he was 78. Davis died in 1990, only 64 years old. None of the five Rat Packers remain to embellish the tales. MacLaine does, but she has said what she will say.

FAS

Dean
The Songs
of
LESLIE BRICUSSE

BETTMANN/GETTY

IT WASN'T THE SAME, it couldn't possibly have been the same. They were older, and Martin, in particular, wasn't into it. When they had announced the tour at Chasen's restaurant in Los Angeles in December 1987, he had joked about calling the whole thing off right there. But Sinatra wanted to proceed, not least to help his friend, who was still in grief over the death of his son Dean Paul Martin, in a plane crash in March 1987 on San Gorgonio Mountain—the same site where Sinatra's mother, Dolly, had perished in a plane accident a decade earlier. "I think it would be great for Dean," Sinatra told Davis. "Get him out. For that alone it would be worth doing." He also reportedly told Sammy that his personal take might be as much as $8 million, which was enticing to the financially troubled entertainer. So the tour kicked off in Oakland, but Martin, who hadn't made a movie or recorded a song since 1984 and who was deep into the bottle (on the following pages, that's not apple juice in the glass this time), simply couldn't proceed. He threw a lit cigarette into the audience at one point, and he quit after four shows, claiming kidney problems. The second iteration of the Rat Pack, a mythical entity that had never really had a beginning, was well and truly ended.

NEAL PRESTON

MARTIN, DAVIS and Sinatra in 1988.

"THE ULTIMATE EVENT" became the new name for the erstwhile Rat Pack tour, which continued on after Liza Minnelli, seen here with Sammy and Frank in Rotterdam, was summoned to replace Dean. The substitution was apt in many ways, and certainly resonant for Sinatra: Liza's mother, Judy Garland, had been his tablemate many a time back in the days of Bogie's Holmby Hills Rat Pack. The tour was a great success, not least because Sammy, who didn't have two years left to live, was yet in fine form ("pure, ebullient, unapologetic show business," said the *New York Times* of Davis's performance). Not all was roses; there were allegations that Sinatra's camp was skimming profits. But at tour's end in 1989, Frank gave Sammy a gold watch, and Davis was buried with it the following year. In 1990, Sinatra, solo, went out on another national tour, and then he too retired from the stage. Everything about the Rat Pack was now memories.

ROB VERHORST/HOLLANDSE HOOGTE/REDUX

JUST ONE MORE

Dean is the headliner at the Sands this night—September 6, 1963. Sammy and Frank are backstage, and suddenly they are onstage. Everyone's happy about this: Dean, Frank, Sammy, especially the audience. Everyone's happy. That's it in a nutshell. That was the Rat Pack experience. That was what it was all about. Happy.

BETTMANN/GETTY

Printed in Poland
by Amazon Fulfillment
Poland Sp. z o.o., Wrocław

50617817R00068